BEYOND SOUL TREK

THE NEXT CHAPTER OF WOMEN'S AWAKENING

PUJA KANKANI

INDIA • SINGAPORE • MALAYSIA

ISBN

Paperback: 979-8-89133-951-4

Hardcase: 979-8-89186-538-9

Dedication

To My Dearest Mother,

For your unwavering love, boundless strength, and the countless lessons in resilience and grace that you've bestowed upon me. You are the embodiment of empowerment, and this book stands as a tribute to your enduring influence on my life.

To My Incredible Female Readers,

This book is dedicated to each of you—strong, resilient, and remarkable. May the words within these pages empower you to embark on your own soul trek, to discover the boundless strength within, and to illuminate your path with courage and purpose. Together, we rise.

With love and gratitude,

Puja Kankani

CONTENTS

ACKNOWLEDGMENTS

First and foremost, I extend my heartfelt gratitude to the Divine for bestowing upon me the privilege of penning this book, allowing me to share the life skills and wisdom I have gathered through the years and diverse experiences.

To my unwavering pillars of strength, my beloved parents, **Ms. Nirmala Kankani** and **Mr. Srigopal Kankani**, your trust in my abilities has exceeded my own belief in myself throughout this journey. My mother, in particular, stands as an enduring and towering presence in my life.

My son, **Naman Kankani**, your presence has been an unshakable source of strength, propelling my achievements and enhancing my capabilities.

Gratitude extends to my revered Gurus and cherished friends, who have offered unwavering support in every conceivable way.

In this journey called life, I have been profoundly influenced and motivated by remarkable individuals, including spiritual luminaries such as **Sri Sri Ravishankar, Sadhguru Jaggi Vasudev, BK Shivani, and Gaur Gopal Das.**

From my inner circle, I must mention **Dr. Vijay Prakash**, whose mentorship, both personally and professionally, and his book on financial independence have been transformative.

Mr. Manoj Kumar Singh, your pivotal role in easing the trials of life and your unwavering support during my toughest moments have not gone unnoticed. I extend my sincere thanks for your trust, respect, and support.

To my dear friends, **Ms. Priya and Mr.Piyush Jain**, your unwavering emotional and physical support has been a constant presence in my journey.

Among the beautiful souls I've encountered, two friends hold a special place in my heart: **Ms. Varsha Srivastava** and **Ms. Pratishtha Srivastava.**

The sacred wisdom of **"The Bhagavad Gita"** has played an essential role in guiding me through life's challenges and empowering me to face them with strength.

Last but not least, I express gratitude to myself, for nurturing self-motivation and self-love. My aspiration to inspire others and make a meaningful impact on this planet fuels my existence.

With profound thanks and immense appreciation,

– Puja Kankani

FORWORD

You are about to go on a journey of deep proportions in the pages that follow, one that extends far beyond the difficult routes, the stunning landscapes, and even the uplifting tale of two women on a trek. Every woman has untapped strength, and "Beyond Soul Trek: A Journey into Women's Empowerment" is more than a book—it's a beacon, a source of empowerment, and a celebration of that strength.

Women have always been pillars of strength, silently bearing the burden of a changing world. They have persevered over overwhelming obstacles to carry the flame of change, spark revolutions, and nurture dreams. The purpose of this book is to celebrate such fortitude, perseverance, and insight. We risk challenging accepted wisdom by removing preconceived notions and removing barriers to get to the core of what it means to empower women.

The hike is a metaphor for life, a road we must all travel in our own unique ways. It's a metaphor for life's difficulties, the rewards of tenacity, and the glory of success. This voyage is symbolic of life itself; it's a chance to learn about ourselves, develop as individuals, and tap into our immense latent potential at every turn.

Keep in mind while you read this tale that achieving one's potential isn't limited to a certain gender or set of actions. It is an all-encompassing power that cannot be contained. It's about realizing that power isn't about dominating others, but rather about exercising agency over one's own life and the environment around them.

This book is an open call to take a journey within yourself. It's a challenge to figure out what makes you special, to accept yourself as you are, and to use that to make a difference in the world. You will discover wisdom, inspiration, and direction inside these pages whether you are a woman seeking empowerment, a man eager to understand and support the women in your life, or just someone interested about the tremendous strength of the human spirit.

Dear reader, as you flip through the pages of "Beyond Soul Trek," may the tales and advice you find there guide you. May they shed light on your road, stoke your inner fire, and give you the confidence to explore the world beyond your wildest dreams; for the way to personal growth and development is not found in a book, but rather in the actions you perform, the relationships you cultivate, and the lives you touch.

With unbounded optimism and unyielding faith,

Dr. Vijay Prakash

#1 Bestselling Author of SLUMDOG INVESTOR

AUTHOR BIO

Puja Kankani's journey through life is a remarkable testament to resilience, determination, and the unyielding belief in the power of one's dreams. With an MBA to her name, she has not only scaled the heights of success in the corporate world but has also emerged as a guiding light for those fortunate enough to know her.

In her professional life, Puja is a shining star in a leading IT firm. Her dedication and hard work have not only propelled her career but have also inspired countless colleagues and peers. Puja's journey through the corporate landscape is a testament to her unwavering commitment to excellence.

However, Puja's story is not confined to the boardroom. She is a multi-faceted individual with a deep passion for the arts and adventure. From her early days, Puja has graced theatre stages with her presence, captivating audiences with her dance performances. Her love for the arts is a testament to her creative spirit and her ability to express herself through movement and expression.

But Puja's interests don't end there. She is an enthusiast of a multitude of activities, from cycling to yoga, from athletics to adventure. Her boundless energy and curiosity drive her to explore new horizons, both in the physical and spiritual realms. Puja's commitment to maintaining a healthy and active lifestyle is an inspiration to those around her.

One of Puja's most remarkable qualities is her love for travel. She is a globetrotter at heart, always seeking new destinations to explore. Her wanderlust has taken her to the far corners of the globe, allowing her to immerse herself in diverse cultures and cuisines. Puja's passion for travel is not merely about seeing new places; it's about connecting with the world, understanding its beauty, and savoring the local vegetarian delicacies that each destination has to offer.

Through her writings, Puja aspires to share the wealth of experiences, insights, and wisdom she has accumulated over the years. Her words are not just a reflection of her own journey but a source of inspiration for others seeking to navigate the complexities of life with grace and determination.

Puja Kankani is more than a name; she is a living embodiment of the belief that with resilience, determination, and an unwavering commitment to one's passions, there are no limits to what one can achieve. Her story serves as a beacon of hope and a reminder that the human spirit, when ignited by passion and fueled by perseverance, can illuminate even the darkest of paths. Puja's journey is a testament to the boundless potential that resides within each of us, waiting to be unleashed.

WHAT INSPIRED ME TO INK THIS BOOK?

While we worship deities like Goddess Durga and Goddess Saraswati, women often face disparities starting from childhood. The other day, I was in the temple when a shriek invaded my ears. As I turned around, I noticed a middle-aged man growling at his wife. Getting distracted from my prayers, my mind tuned in to the frequency of the boiling words. After a few moments, I gathered that the wife had forgotten to carry the flower petals. The irate man commanded his wife to hop through the tall stairs and bring him his flowers as if those were the magic wand to please God.

All this while, the father and mother of this man looked at their daughter-in-law as a sinner. Whereas the two juveniles (a son and a daughter) gaped at their mother with pitiful eyes. Most likely, upon growing up, the boy would follow in the footsteps of his father the daughter her mother's. Is it always the duty of a woman to mend broken ends? Is this not slavery?

As the 'obedient' wife returned with bated breath and sweating profusely, she noticed her husband lying in obeisance in front of the idol of Goddess Lakshmi. After his mantra recitation, he got up and swirled the flowers at the idol as if they would get transported to the abode of the goddess, and she would grant him his every wish. I do not want to challenge anyone's devotion, but this is the bitter truth that prevails.

Here are some dialects that we often hear at some point in our lives:

Little Diya: Mom, Ryan always gobbles his chocolates and then mine too.

Mom (from the kitchen): It is okay, Diya; learn to share.

Little Diya: But mom, Ryan never shares his toys.

Mom: Diya, girls are supposed to play with dolls, not toys.

After some years...

Little Diya: Dad, I want to be a scientist and join the ISRO (Indian Space Research Organization).

Dad: Diya, how many female scientists do you know of? Isaac Newton, Albert Einstein, Charles David, and Thomas Edison were all men. Girls learn about household work, complete their graduation, and get married.

Diya: The time has changed Dad, what never happened in past does not mean it cannot happen in the future.

Mom: Diya, now you sound arrogant, girls must abide by some boundaries.

Dad: You better focus on your studies and learn some recipes from mom.

After some more years...

Diya: Mom and dad, now I am a working woman, but I have no plans for marriage until I get promoted to the senior level. Moreover, I do not want to tie a knot with a stranger. We both should first know if we are compatible with each other. After all, it is a question of our and many more lives connected with us.

Dad (mournful, as if someone has passed away at home): Diya, you have disappointed me. Are these the moral values we have taught you? Your mom and I did not know each other before marriage, but we are still together. Do you think your mom is unhappy?

Diya (self-talking): Dad, if you look into mom's eyes, you will get your answer. I have known her only as an embodiment of sacrifice.

There is no denying the fact that gender disparities exist in various areas of life. These could be in employment opportunities, wages, or career progression. The gender pay gap, where women earn less than men for performing similar work, is a pervasive issue in many countries. Women also tend to be overrepresented in lower-paying occupations and underrepresented in leadership positions.

We all talk about gender equality, women's empowerment, women's upliftment, and what not. But are we really implementing all of those that go into these kinds of talks? While there have been several girl welfare programs running globally, inequality still exists. Factors such as poverty, cultural norms, and early marriage can limit girls' access to quality education. Women's education is vital for empowering them economically, socially, and politically.

Therefore, through this book, I intend to raise awareness and encourage others to challenge and overcome gender biases. While we rely on governments and organizations to reform policies, I think we individuals also have a paramount role to play. So, this self-help book is my small and humble contribution to the upliftment of society.

Helping others reach their full potential animates me. So, I intend to provide guidance, inspiration, and practical tools for personal and professional growth.

I feel a deep desire to challenge the status quo and contribute to creating a more equitable and inclusive society. Therefore, my objective is to share general concerns, propose solutions, and inspire you to take action.

This book is on women's empowerment; however, quoting that it is only for females is an understatement. This can help you become aware of the mindset of a female and understand that we are all born humans. So, humanity and prosperity should be our first codes of conduct, not gender inequality. And we can do so by shadowing each other.

I have always been inspired by women like Mary Kom, Oprah Winfrey, and many more who have made significant contributions to society. Therefore, I have shared some real-life examples to amplify their voices. Plus, there are learnings and proven tools knitted into a story. The book takes you on a journey full of sky-soaring peaks and plunging troughs.

So, let us get set go.

Chapter 1

STUCK IN THE RUT

"It is often the small steps, not the giant leaps, that bring about the most lasting change."

– Queen Elizabeth II

The Dawn of Transformation

It's 4 AM on a bitterly cold day in October. The divinities are taking a dip in the spine-freezing Satopanth Tal. This holy lake is situated 14,000 feet above sea level amidst the ice-capped peaks of Uttarakhand. Towards the northern hemisphere, Lord Sun, dressed in radiant jewels, is all set to step into His chariot with His infinite reservoir of luminance. The chariot is chaperoned by seven horses: Gayatri, Brihati, Ushnih, Jagati, Trishtubha, Anushtubha and Pankti,as white as the driven snow.

Humanity is unaware of these celestial eventualities and is slumbering like a toddler, sandwiched in thick blankets. It is only the yogis and the travelers who are awake at this hour of dawn. The sages are keen to spend this time meditating and praying to their gods. Whereas, the explorers are enthused to be all eyes on the picturesque scenery, taking a break from the hustle and bustle of life. The motive of both human species is one: to achieve contentment. For one, it is the quest for perennial fulfillment and temporary gratification; for the other.

The valley is silent except for the melodious chirping of the birds, when suddenly a rip-roaring sound unsettles the stillness. It is the cacophony of an SUV engine on an uphill climb, followed by another and then another. The trail of cars pulls the brakes as they ascend to the foothills. Smiles and raised hands could be seen as they took a gander at the flora and fauna around them. These are seekers from different parts of the country who enrolled online for a trekking journey. As they treat their eyes and souls with the majestic sights, the leader of the camp, Jayesh, voices while ticking off the list, "Hey, where is Maya? She was behind us. I do not see her car. There were two more female members with her when we hit the road from Rishikesh."

As everyone looks at each other with blank expressions, they suddenly notice a car a few feet in the air, landing with a creak and racing towards them. The counter in the speedometer is still at a constant. The rolling tires rally to the parking area and take a 180-degree spin before coming to a screeching halt. Amidst the whirl of dust, the occupants get down with their hearts thumping against their ribcages. One of the co-passengers utters, "Maya is a daredevil driver. We got late because, a few kilometers back, she spotted a snow leopard prowling on the side lane. So, she pulled over, laying her hands on her DSLR and clicking pictures. Whereas, we watched her from the rolled-up windows with bated breaths."

Silence prevails as Maya, a woman in her early forties, gets down from the driver's seat, untying and then retying her hair.

She walks to the boot of the car to take out her camping bag. Jayesh introduces the new member to the rest of the team. As Maya shakes hands with Jiya, she pauses for a moment as she finds her face familiar and vice versa. But as the journey is long, they would have ample time to dig out any past connections.

Maya sweeps around and returns, "Hey, are you Jiya from Christ College, Bangalore?

Jiya's wearing a too-tight sweater. She smiles and replies, "Yes, and I remember we were classmates, but with different groups in the class."

Maya: What a pleasant surprise to see you here. The world is small, right?

Jiya: Yes, it was my pleasure to meet you too, and it has been ages, and you are much more glowing now!

Maya: If I remember it right, you belong to a rich business family, and you got married to a business tycoon. Ah! You were born with a silver spoon. Lucky you! Well, it's great to be a part of this adventure, and it's nice to meet you after so long.

In front of them lies the treacherous range of the Bali Pass Trek, located 16,250 feet above sea level. The journey is going to be full of perils, as there have been instances of avalanches, and November is one of the riskiest months to hike.

As the team prepares to dive into the trekking gear, Jiya, not able to hold her curiosity anymore, asks Maya, "Where are you from?"

Maya: "Currently, I am working with a corporate company in Bangalore, leading the analytics team."

Jiya: "That's great to know! As much as I can recall from our college days, you were always a jolly and bubbly person."

Maya: "Yes, I always wore a smile on my face, as I am a person who doesn't share the pain I go through, and I do not let anyone know this. When you have to fight for almost everything as a girl, your confidence gets trashed, and you lose yourself. And this is exactly what happened to me. Hence, I was low on confidence."

Jiya: "Who would say this looking at you now? I am witnessing a girl with hot-off-the-fire confidence. Wow! What a transformation!"

Meanwhile, Jayesh claps, seeking everyone's attention. "Dear all twelve seekers, I hope you guys have rested well. (Turning around and pointing towards a nearby valley.) The cluster of houses that you see is village Sankri. This tiny hamlet is the last roadhead to this trekking site. (Turning back) Now what you see in front of your eyes is the white-washed trek route to the Bali Pass. For the next eight days, you won't find any shopping malls, finger-licking burger outlets, the comfort of your homes, or even the cuddles of your family members. Rather, you will be eyeball-to-eyeball with the barbarous uphill terrain, unfriendly weather, carnivorous wildlife as your stalking companions, caves (not luxury hotels) to seek shelter, a limited food supply, and many more.

However, I assure you, this is a once-in-a-lifetime experience. The memories of this expedition will remain etched in the folder of your memories for a long time, if not forever. Once you reach the summit, there will be no standing ovations, but what you will experience dwarfs any accolade made by mankind: contentment!

Also, two local helpers will be carrying the food supplies, first aid, and other equipment we might need on the way. They might be here any minute.

I am assuming that you have been doing the workouts as suggested on our website. This will help you outrun and heal speedily from the fatigue, which will be your mate on this journey.

After all, this is the hike you all have been waiting for weeks, so let's kick off and unfold one of the best trips of your life.

Oh, I forgot to mention: normally, there is a team of 12 members who leave from this point, but only 7-8 have it to pass. Others have to return because of some injury, or they surrender to adversity. However, I am hoping that this time, we all (12) will make it to the end of the line.

So, cheers to everyone; we will leave in another five minutes."

As Jayesh completes his little-stretched speech, everyone looks at each other bewildered. Amidst the wave of excitement, another tide prevails, which is one of fright. But this medley is missing from Maya's face. She is ecstatic to the brim.

With the bags hung to their backs, the departure whistle blows.

While all the team members footslog across the narrow pathway, Maya and Jiya trail to the end of the queue.

Jiya: I am still eager to hear your reply, Maya. What is the reason behind such a pronounced makeover?"

Maya (with a smile): Well, if I time-traveled to the flashback—not too far, just a year or two back—I would never have imagined that I would be going on this challenging trek ever in my life. I was living in a shell, in my own small world jam-packed with herculean challenges and scarce moments of joy. The obstacles are still there, but the only difference is that I am now equipped with the tools to handle them.

Jiya: I am curious to know about those methodologies. Most people hypothesize that being born into a rich family is a boon, as you have all the luxuries at your fingertips.

As a single child, I had all the privileges that the middle class is deprived of. A chauffeur-driven car for the pick-up and drop-off, palatable cuisine in the lunch box, choicest tuitions, followed by lawn tennis and swimming classes alternatively in the evenings Where, for other kids, summer vacations were limited to visiting granny's house or a hill station for a couple of days, my parents took me to exotic locations out of the country. Besides, there was a band of household helpers managing the chores. I was never bothered about my future.

However, gradually, I started bumping into other realities of life. As there was no dearth of money, I became a spendthrift, not knowing the value of money. I became a part of groups where bragging, condemning, smoking, and drinking were status symbols. This drifted me apart from my family.

Then one day, my parents informed me they had arranged my marriage with the son of a family friend. I resisted as I was not mentally prepared yet, but my mother insisted that the boy was from an opulent family and I would be living an even more extravagant life. I did not know that the main reason behind that alliance was monetizing a business partnership. The marriage was arranged with bells and whistles.

But as they say, honeymoons are short-lived, so soon I found myself waiting for my husband at the dinner table and then dozing off. Busy in his meetings and collaborations, he seldom had any time for me. Then, after two years, when I gave birth to a baby girl, I thought our angel would be the source of rebounding the ties, but things continued to be the same.

Now, it has been eight years since our marriage, and we are well on our way to divorce. I have thought that after I return from this voyage, I will break the news of my separation from my husband.

Maya: "Oh! This is saddening. I can very well relate to you, as I have been through similar face-offs. I have faced enough as a girl. How I wish we had the choice to be born a girl or a boy! My story goes below."

Childhood is to play, not to learn about inequality

It was raining cats and dogs, and a mother who was experiencing severe labor pains was being rushed to the hospital, which was at a distance from the village. Fortunately, the hospital van arrived well on time, and the mother was ferried along with some family members. As the van snaked to the porch of the hospital, two nurses bustled toward the door and helped the mother lie on a stretcher. Suddenly, the silent layers of air outside the delivery room get penetrated by the ear-splitting cries of a baby. The mother looked at the baby with graying eyes, not because of the pain but because of the euphoria of bringing another life to this earth.

However, the environment on the other side of the wall was not as animated. There were whispers among the family members, "It's a girl again." However, for the mother, though this was her third child, the joy was still boundless.

In the year 1989, the family relocated from North East India to South India, all the way from Assam to Bangalore (now known as Bengaluru), the Green City. The girl is a 3-year-old toddler now. Yes, the girl here is me, but this story could be yours too.

My schooling started in Bangalore, but I was not very school-friendly. Every morning, I would see my brother Dhruv and sister Tina getting ready for school with a wave of excitement, but I was averse to leaving my family.

Being from the middle-class strata, affording a car was something extra-terrestrial for our budget. So, after tucking the bags and lunch boxes to the sides of the scooter, my father would pilot Dhruv, Tina, and me to the school. Upon reaching, I would wail every single day, trying to clutch my father's legs. He would try to quieten me down by intonating, "It's just a matter of a few hours. You study well, and I will come to fetch you in the afternoon. Then, turning to my siblings, he would utter, "Take care of Maya." Dhruv and Tina were older than me by 4 and 2 years, respectively, and they would handhold me to my classroom. While walking past the gate of the school, they would keep turning back and waving to my dad, and I would be busy bawling at the top of my lungs. Even the yummiest of the candy invented by mankind could not stop me from crying at that time.

However, as I grew up, I started to develop a liking for school. I too would wave goodbye to Dad with a cheek-to-cheek smile. As a self-effacing kid, I turned amicable and had a keen eye for sports and dance. I won several inter-school tournaments in athletics.

The societal impediment

When I was turning 18, I was endowed with a marvelous opportunity to perform Indian folk dance in front of a vast crowd in Bengaluru. It was a Rajasthani dance, and I had to perform while balancing eleven pots over my head. The platform was covered with broken glass pieces and nails. My mother was a key chairperson of the community society that organized the show, of which I was a part. I can still recall the echo of clapping and standing ovations after my performance.

However, despite the merriment on the outside, there was an internal war on the inside. Since the time I was born, Tina has had to make sacrifices. Even though she was a kid, she had to play the role of my guardian. When she wished to play outside with the girls of her age, she was asked to attend to me. On most occasions, she was reluctant, but she had no other choice. Then, as she became a teenager, her young ears were instructed to learn the household chores. And later, even I was asked to follow suit. Although I was the youngest, I was given a little leverage; I felt bad for Tina. However, Dhruv was completely devoid of responsibilities.

Why?

Because he was a boy. Household work is only meant for girls. Yes, this gender inequality exists in society even today. And I do not blame my parents for this. Their parents instilled this gender disparity in them, and their parents in turn carried on this legacy from their parents. It is not the generations that are to be held responsible, but the conservative mindset.

This led me to the resolve that I would not hammer the same ideology into the upcoming generation.

At the age of 18, like any other kid, even though I wanted to live life at full throttle, I aspired to travel around, make friends, and fly like a bird in the infinite sky. But my feet were barbwired by societal obligations, and Tina's situation was no different. On the contrary, Dhruv was allowed to go on trips with male and female friends and, at times, even return home late.

We might claim to be from a modernistic era with smart technology on our palmtops. However, we are still marching with the rock of gender differentiation anchored to our feet. I come across several people who deliver awe-inspiring speeches on gender equality, but behind the closed walls, they are the brand ambassadors of boy-girl disparity.

Since childhood, we girls have been taught to adjust, sacrifice, not argue, take care of domestic chores, and many more. And there is nothing wrong with acquiring these attributes. Anything that strengthens family ties is worthy of learning. But why are boys not coached on the same building blocks? Is that because if they too learned the same traits, they would not be demanding anymore? Would they no longer be the contenders for the head of the family? Well, this is nothing but the wild weed growth of a limiting mindset.

We are often fed with:

- You are a girl, so it is only you who is responsible for the household chores.
- Focus on your studies and fetch good grades—not for a job, but to find a good match. Highly educated girls are preferred the most.

- Being a woman, it's your basic call of duty to cook, clean, and take care of children.
- Even if your husband does not care for you, you must not endanger your marriage, or what will society say? Single or separated women are a curse to society.
- You are a woman; you can pursue your career only if your husband permits.

And the list is endless.

The irony is that most of these statements come from women, particularly mothers.

Do you think that a life lived on someone else's terms is worthy? There is a term called self-dignity. Should every individual not be respected for who she or he is? Should we be at the mercy of others for approval?

Why are men not taught to take care of the home? Why are they not coached to live in collaboration and not in dominance?

The role of a mother is known to be the most responsible job on this planet. I am sure you must have watched the video where a couple of people are interviewed for a vacancy with no holidays, 24/7 availability, no likeliness of appreciation, and, most importantly, no remuneration. Thinking of it as a prank, most people giggle and say, who would do such a job with no day (and night) off, gratitude, and a promotion? When the jaw-dropped interviewees inquire about the profile, the interviewer says it is the job of 'a mother'.

So, back then, I started to chew over why it is that we are not taught to be bold or fighters, or why I am not sent to kickboxing, karate, or self-defense coaching but rather restricted to the boundaries of the house. In-fact, I wanted to pursue my career as a dancer, but my grandfather said "Girls of our family are not dancers and will never be". So, I crushed my dream of becoming a Dancer. However, the answers remained clouded. Moreover, did it even matter? We all know about environmental pollution, and we are aware of the answers as well. We rarely plant a tree or commute via public transport. We are more comfortable laying a guilt trip on the policies, the government, and every single person on the road.

However, the answers had to unfold a couple of years later—the ones that could make a difference.

Here, I might sound rebellious, but in no way do I intend to demean the clan of parents, men, society, or any individual. I am not in favor of crossing swords with the opposite gender or seeking any ill means to fight injustice. Female inequality has been rustling our society for ages, and there must be a prosperous way to combat this limiting mindset. Eye for eye is by no means a solution to any problem.

Disparity on the job front

When I landed my first job as a project associate, I was excited to embark on my professional journey. Little did I know that I would soon face a multitude of challenges that most females often encounter in the office.

I worked tirelessly to establish a successful career at a prestigious corporate firm. However, I soon found myself bumping into a battalion of challenges that most females encounter in the office.

As a woman, I've observed that some men may exhibit a sense of entitlement and attempt to assert dominance over me. Regrettably, I've encountered situations where certain male colleagues and my boss have acted unprofessionally, demonstrating a lack of restraint and respect. Their behavior often crosses boundaries, and when women assert themselves, it appears to challenge their ego, in turn hampering professional growth of a women.

The first one was the subtle but pervasive gender bias. Despite my qualifications and expertise, I noticed that my contributions were often overlooked or attributed to my male colleagues. This bias hindered my professional growth and made me feel undervalued.

I found that I was consistently earning less than my male counterparts who held similar positions. The gender pay-scale gap was not only disheartening but also added to my financial pressures.

Most of us aspire to climb the corporate ladder, and so do I. But I encountered the notorious "glass ceiling." Promotions seemed elusive, and I witnessed the stark underrepresentation of women in leadership positions. The lack of female role models and mentors made it challenging for me to envision my path to success.

Moreover, I struggled with work-life balance. The demanding nature of my job made it difficult for me to fulfill my personal responsibilities. I had to miss many birthdays and other occasions in the family to meet the deadlines at work. The expectations society placed on me as a woman to manage both work and home often left me feeling overwhelmed and stretched thin.

Giving the remote control of your life to others

Why is it that women are not the decision-makers in their own lives before marriage or after marriage? It was never that I could decide and execute anything. I wanted to be a dancer in my profession; I wanted to pursue a diploma in dance; I wished to do an MBA from a renowned university like IIM, ISB, or something of similar standards; and many more to list. I was just not permitted to do these. Really PERMITTED. Do we need permission to breathe or to live? I did my MBA at a very normal college, and there I happened to get into a relationship with my male friend, and I was severely punished for this. We wanted to spend life together, and I was not permitted to do so as I didn't have the right to make any decisions of my own. We both were torn apart on religious grounds, and we still lived for 7 years in the hope that the family would agree to get us along. At last, I had to make some decisions in my life, and I chose my family over my happiness and over my feelings. I finally got married to a person working for a corporation.

Is marriage not supposed to be a union of two hearts?

One of the first difficulties I encountered was the expectation to conform to traditional gender roles. Society had ingrained in me the notion that I should be the primary caregiver and responsible for managing household chores and childcare. This put a significant burden on me as I juggled my professional aspirations and household responsibilities.

With time, I also realized that my career progression took a backseat after marriage. While I dwelled on my dreams and ambitions, societal expectations and family pressures often pushed me to prioritize my husband's career and the needs of our growing family. I wrestled to find a balance between my aspirations and fulfilling the traditional role of a wife.

Sometimes, I felt that my identity and independence were suffocating. The transition from being an independent woman to being part of a married unit sometimes meant compromising my ambitions. I often felt that my voice and opinions were not given the same weight as my husband's, leading to a sense of disempowerment.

Communication breakdowns, conflicts, and the unequal distribution of household responsibilities created tension and strain. The societal expectations of being the peacemaker and maintaining harmony in the relationship added further pressure on me.

Furthermore, I experienced the emotional toll of constantly comparing myself to the societal ideals of the "perfect wife." I felt the weight of expectations to be beautiful, nurturing, and always available to cater to my husband's needs. This constant pressure to meet unrealistic standards often made me question my self-worth.

Chapter 2

STAY STRONG AND LIVE LONG

"To keep the body in good health is a duty; otherwise, we shall not be able to keep our mind strong and clear."

– Buddha

As the crew heads to the Chilurgad trek, it starts to drizzle. So, they decide to slurp some tea at a miniature tea stall on the walkway. Holding the piping hot cups, the trekkers take an eyeful of the splendid panorama. The view was clearer than the most elegant HD TV could relay. Everything around, even the spade of grass, looks brand new after soaking in the pour. The aroma could easily triumph over the most mesmerizing perfume ever created. The spectrum of flora and fauna seems to be the landscape's ornaments that could blanch the jewels ever worn by the richest bride on this planet. The gargling waterfalls could beat the priciest organic waters manufactured by mankind. The flowers next to these aquarium-blue waterfalls are nodding gently.

Down the hill, they could see a meadow and a gem-blue stream flowing ceaselessly, hopping over the timeworn rocks happily. Babbling and burbling, it seems like the river is chorusing, 'No matter what comes your way, keep moving forward'. Birds of beautiful feathers fly about its banks and sing merrily.

The fluttering butterflies drifted around the hikers lazily. The hedgerows are pregnant with different fruits. In the front, the heaven-touching apex of the mountains could be seen, wrapped completely in milky-white snow. Everyone is charmed by the beauty of nature.

After a few minutes, the slight downpour ceases, and the 12 trekkers buckle up to resume their journey on the narrow pathway. As they are about to leave, one of the crew members, Rayan, feels severe pain in his leg and tumbles to the ground. The fellow members hustle to pick him up and settle him on a chair. Jayesh, the camp leader, barges in to take stock of the situation.

Jayesh- Rayan, my friend, a cramp seems to have gotten the better of you. Let me give you a leg massage along with this fast-action spray, and you will feel relieved.

However, even after resting for 15 minutes, Rayan could feel no improvement.

Jayesh- Bro, I do not think you are fit to continue further. You should backtrack, and I am sending a helper with you.

With all eyes on the turn of events, Maya steps in.

Maya-Rayan, you are a brave boy, and courageous people do not give up. So, let's try one more time, and I am sure it will bring respite to your muscle pull. This could be a little challenging, but we are here to outrun the challenges, aren't we?

Saying this, she drops her bag and gets into a tabletop posture, asking Rayan to follow her. She extends her right leg back, lifting it off the ground in line with her lower back.

Maya: Stay in this position; else, if comfortable, raise your left hand out as well, so you are balancing on two limbs. Pull the navel towards the spine so your core is engaged and you are not sinking at the lower back. Hold for 5 to 9 breaths, and then switch sides.

Then Rayan gets back to his feet. After limping for a few steps, he gets his normal walking posture back, as if no cramp ever surfaced. Rayan turns back and flashes a smile that could sell a million magazine covers. Then he gives her a thumbs up, voicing a loud 'thank you, Maya and let's move on'. With side-splitting laughter, everyone claps for Maya, clutching their bags on their backs and sticks in their hands.

Jayesh- This is marvelous, Maya. I have been a guide for 15 years, but I never knew about this yogic remedy. What is this called, anyway?

Maya- This is Dwipada Marajriasana (Bird Dog Balance). I often practiced this when I got muscle tension during my sports days in school. And this has worked wonders for me so far.

Jayesh- Bravo Maya. I think I should also practice this, as cramps are likely to happen while trekking.

The team makes inroads to the incline like ants in the hunt for their day's sugar ball.

Jiya- Wow, Maya, you look like a fitness freak. Health is a domain I always struggle with. Can you please mentor me on how I can stay fit as a fiddle?

Maya- Sure. This reminds me of a wonderful quote.

"Take care of your body. It is the only place you have to live."

– Jim Rohn

The credit goes to my parents, who ingrained in me the habit of staying fit. Most people think of first earning wealth and then health. If you are not healthy, you cannot enjoy the wealth you have accumulated. Becoming health-conscious is not a goal but should be a way of life.

Health is incredibly important, as it affects all aspects of our lives. Here are some reasons why health is imperative:

Quality of life: Good health leads to a better quality of life. When we are healthy, we are able to enjoy life more fully, pursue our interests and hobbies, and engage with our communities.

Physical fitness: Maintaining good health enables us to be physically fit and able to perform daily activities without fatigue or discomfort. This can help us maintain independence and mobility as we age.

Mental well-being: Good health can also lead to better mental health, including lower levels of stress, anxiety, and depression. Mental well-being is crucial for our overall happiness and satisfaction in life.

Productivity: Being healthy can also lead to increased productivity, both at work and at home. When we are not feeling well, we may be less productive and have difficulty completing tasks.

Lower healthcare costs: By taking care of our health, we can prevent or manage chronic conditions, which can lead to lower healthcare costs in the long run.

Overall, good health is essential for a happy and fulfilling life, and it is important to prioritize our health through regular exercise, healthy eating habits, and preventive care.

Get in the groove of exercising

Exercising every day is one of the best ways to improve your health. Here are some benefits of exercise:

Improved cardiovascular health: Exercise helps to strengthen the heart and lungs, leading to improved cardiovascular health. This can help reduce the risk of heart disease, stroke, and other chronic conditions.

Better mental health: Exercise has been shown to improve mental health by reducing symptoms of anxiety and depression and improving self-esteem and mood.

Increased muscle strength and flexibility: Exercise helps to build muscle and improve flexibility, which can help prevent injuries and improve overall physical performance.

Weight management: Regular exercise can help you maintain a healthy weight or lose weight by burning calories and building muscle.

Reduced risk of chronic diseases: Exercise has been linked to a reduced risk of chronic diseases such as diabetes, cancer, and osteoporosis.

Some examples of exercises include:

Aerobic exercise: Examples include running, cycling, swimming, or brisk walking. Aim for at least 150 minutes of moderate-intensity aerobic exercise per week.

Strength training: Examples include lifting weights or using resistance bands. Aim for two or more strength training sessions per week.

Flexibility and balance exercises: Examples include yoga, morning walks, or stretching. Incorporate these exercises into your routine to improve balance and flexibility.

Start slowly and gradually increase the intensity and duration of your exercise routine. It's also important to consult with your healthcare provider before starting a new exercise program, especially if you have any pre-existing medical conditions.

Jiya- This is concise and informative. However, forming a routine is what I often lock horns with. This year, I resolved to wake up early and get into my jogging shoes. I set up an alarm for 5:30 am and bingo; I was at the gate of the nearby park at 5:45 am. That day, I was energetic for the entire day and completed all my tasks on time. Not only physically, but even my mind was also rejuvenated, as you have mentioned about better mental health.

But it is the human tendency to switch back to the comfort zone. Your mind always keeps you away from doing something challenging and forming new life-nourishing habits. By the end of January, I would snooze the alarm several times and even sandwich my head between pillows. And by the first week of February, I did not bother even setting an alarm. Are there some hacks you can help me with to stick to the routine?

Maya- Of course, our minds have been programmed to backpedal to our comfort zone. This reminds me of another quote.

"The mind is a wonderful servant, but a terrible master."

– Robin Sharma

Why are humans more prone to unhealthy habits?

Because:

- They require less effort.
- They provide a significant reward.
- They give instant gratification (immediate pleasure).

You need very little effort to keep watching TV, YouTube, or Netflix for long hours. You feel free from stress instantly when you do that.

So, here are some tips to tame your mind for creating an exercise routine:

Set realistic goals: Start by setting achievable goals that are specific, measurable, and realistic. For example, aim to exercise for 30 minutes a day, three times a week.

Choose activities you enjoy: Choose activities that you enjoy and that fit your fitness level and interests. This will make it more likely that you stick with your routine.

Mix it up: Incorporate a variety of exercises into your routine, including cardio, strength training, and flexibility exercises. This can help keep your workouts interesting and prevent boredom.

Schedule your workouts: Schedule your workouts at a consistent time each day or week, and treat them like any other appointment. This can help make exercise a habit.

Start slowly: If you are new to exercise, start slowly and gradually increase the intensity and duration of your workouts. This can help prevent injuries and ensure that you don't get discouraged.

Track your progress: Keep track of your workouts and progress over time, such as by using a fitness tracker or journal. This can help you stay motivated and see the improvements you have made.

Deena Kastor is a long-distance runner who has won numerous accolades and set several records in her career. However, her journey to becoming a world-class athlete was not without its challenges.

Deena grew up in a small town in California and began running in high school. She showed promise and earned a scholarship to run at the University of Arkansas. However, during her freshman year, she suffered a stress fracture in her foot that left her unable to compete for months.

Despite the setback, Deena remained determined to become a great runner. She worked hard to rehab her injury and began training again. She soon began setting personal bests and winning races.

In 2004, Deena qualified for the Olympic Games in Athens. She went on to win the bronze medal in the marathon, becoming the first American woman to medal in the event in 20 years. She also set the American record in the marathon with a time of 2:19:36.

Deena continued to compete at a high level for several years, winning several major races and setting records along the way. However, she faced another setback in 2008 when she suffered a stress fracture in her back. She was forced to take a break from running and focus on rehab.

Despite the injury, Deena remained committed to her training and returned to competition stronger than ever. In 2014, she won the Chicago Marathon at the age of 41, becoming the oldest woman to win a major marathon.

Deena's story shows us the power of perseverance and dedication to exercising. Despite facing several setbacks and injuries throughout her career, she remained focused on her goals and worked hard to overcome obstacles. Her success serves as an inspiration to many and shows us that with the right mindset and determination, we can accomplish incredible things.

Remember, any physical activity is better than none, so even small amounts of exercise can be beneficial. Be patient with yourself and focus on making exercise a sustainable habit over time.

Don't live for eating; eat for living

Healthy eating habits are crucial for maintaining good health and preventing chronic diseases. Here are some tips for developing healthy eating habits:

Eat a variety of nutrient-dense foods: Focus on consuming foods that are nutrient-dense, such as fruits, vegetables, whole grains, lean proteins, and healthy fats. These foods provide essential vitamins, minerals, and other nutrients that support good health.

Limit processed foods: Processed foods are often high in calories, unhealthy fats, and added sugars. Try to limit your intake of processed foods and choose whole foods instead.

Watch your portion sizes: Eating too much, even of healthy foods, can lead to weight gain. Use smaller plates, measure your portions, and be mindful of how much you are eating.

Stay hydrated: Drinking plenty of water is important for maintaining good health. Aim for at least 8–10 glasses of water per day, and limit your intake of sugary drinks.

Avoid skipping meals: Skipping meals can lead to overeating later in the day and can also affect your energy levels. Try to eat three balanced meals per day, and include healthy snacks if needed.

Plan your meals: Planning your meals ahead of time can help you make healthier choices and avoid impulse eating. Try to plan your meals for the week and prepare meals in advance if possible.

Be mindful of your eating habits: Pay attention to your hunger and fullness cues, and try to eat in a calm and relaxed environment. Avoid distractions such as TV or phones while eating.

Make craving distasteful: If you make craving plain-looking, then your mind will not crave the reward, and it will change the routine.

For example, put your snack items in a box and write on top of it in bold letters "**Not Good For Me**". This way, every time you have a craving and reach out to the box, your craving will become unattractive, and your conscious mind will take charge and try to avoid this routine.

If you eat healthy food before going to the market or party, your craving to eat unhealthy food outside will fade.

Get rid of the triggers: If you can manage to remove the trigger or make it invisible, then you can break the habit loop. When your mind doesn't sense the trigger, it will not follow the habit routine.

Let's say you want to get rid of eating snacks at home. You see snack items (triggers) and get a craving for eating. By hiding a snack item where it is not visible frequently, you can make the trigger invisible. This way, you're eating snack frequency will decrease significantly because you will eat only when you have a strong craving.

Avoid going to places where you will see triggers.

Avoid being with people who will expose you to triggers.

Don't let people's positions trigger your surroundings.

Avoid media that shows you triggers.

Remember, healthy eating habits are not about strict rules or deprivation. Instead, focus on making sustainable changes to your diet that you can maintain over time.

Dr. Terry Wahls, a clinical professor of medicine at the University of Iowa, was diagnosed with multiple sclerosis (MS) in 2000. Over the years, her condition worsened, to the point where she was confined to a wheelchair and had to use a tilt-recline wheelchair to move around.

Dr. Wahls was determined to find a way to improve her health and reduce her symptoms, so she began researching the connection between diet and MS. She developed a nutrition plan that focused on nutrient-dense, whole foods and eliminated processed foods, gluten, and dairy.

She also incorporated regular exercise and started practicing stress-reduction techniques like meditation and deep breathing.

Within a few months of adopting this new lifestyle, Dr. Wahls noticed significant improvements in her health. She was able to walk without assistance and was no longer dependent on her wheelchair. Her energy levels increased, and her cognitive function improved.

Dr. Wahls' success with her lifestyle changes inspired her to share her story and educate others on the connection between diet and MS. She wrote a book, "The Wahls Protocol," which details her journey and outlines her nutrition and lifestyle plan.

She continues to practice and teach her lifestyle plan and has helped many others with MS and other chronic illnesses improve their health and quality of life. Her story serves as a reminder that with determination and a willingness to make changes, we can take control of our health and improve our well-being.

The Safety Net of Preventive Care

Preventive care refers to actions you can take to prevent or detect potential health problems before they become more serious. Here are some examples of preventive care:

Regular check-ups and screenings: Regular check-ups with your healthcare provider can help detect potential health problems early on. Your healthcare provider may also recommend certain screenings based on your age, gender, and medical history, such as mammograms, colonoscopies, or blood pressure checks.

Vaccines: Vaccines can help protect you from infectious diseases such as the flu, pneumonia, and HPV. Talk to your healthcare provider about which vaccines are recommended for you based on your age and medical history.

Healthy lifestyle choices: Making healthy lifestyle choices can help prevent chronic diseases and improve your overall health. This includes eating a healthy diet, staying physically active, avoiding tobacco and excessive alcohol consumption, and managing stress.

Managing chronic conditions: If you have a chronic condition such as diabetes, high blood pressure, or asthma, managing it properly can help prevent complications and improve your overall health.

Mental health care: Mental health is just as important as physical health. Seeking mental health care when needed can help prevent more serious problems and improve your quality of life.

By focusing on preventive care, you can help reduce your risk of developing serious health problems and improve your overall health and well-being. Remember to talk to your healthcare provider about which preventive measures are recommended for you based on your age, medical history, and lifestyle.

Jiya- This is wholesome, Maya. Now I know I do not have to look for motivation on the outside and instead be self-inspired by following your suggestions. The best part is that you have not written essays to clarify your point. You have mentioned the pointers in a brief and actionable array.

Maya- Thanks Jiya. I believe what I have shared is something we all know. But, wearing the horse blinders, we get so busy in the hustle of life that we compromise our health only to later become victims of some disorder. In most cases, it is a wake-up call, but in some, it is the last call. So, it is better to be health-friendly today and forever.

Jiya- Golden words. Indeed, I will keep this in mind and let it never fade away.

Meanwhile, they reach the Chilurgad trek, their first destination to set up camp and retire for the day.

Chapter 3

THE ART OF BLOSSOMING YOUR RELATIONSHIPS

"Happily, ever after is not a fairy tale. It's a choice."

– *Fawn Weaver*

At this height of over 9,000 feet, as the moon starts to switch turns with the sun, everyone unpacks their bags and pieces together their tents. Amidst the glorious hues, the clouds are like great wings of gold and yellow. The clarity of the atmosphere and the brilliance of the colors fasten everyone's gaze as the sun waves goodbye for the day. It seems like a canvas painted by the God.

While in one corner, the helpers stew the soup to withstand the icy-cold wind; a few feet away, the trekkers gather around the bonfire. The valley echoes with merriment, singing, dancing, and clapping.

Jiya: Guys, I can say this is the best evening of my life so far. Busy with the chores of my life, I never knew that nature could be this mesmerizing. Looking at the snowscape and serenity, I have forgotten the day's toil to reach here. This spectacle is nothing less than heaven.

But I do not see Jaya and Kartik around.

Aditya (another hiking member) Come on, friends, they are a newly married couple. Plus, the ambiance is the perfect occasion to get into an intimate encounter. So, let's leave them alone with their urges and concentrate on this bonfire.

Megha (another hiking member): No, Aditya, I think the matter is something else. As I was trekking close to them, I could overhear Jaya complaining repeatedly to Kartik for bringing her here. I think she is not used to such arduous undertakings. Kartik was adamant about completing this trek. I think both of them do not want to cast off their ego boundaries.

Jiya (with a mischievous smile): Megha, have you been spying on them?

Taresh (another hiking member): I think Megha is right. Even I heard them getting in a row when we took a break at the tea stall.

Meanwhile, Jayesh walks in, rubbing his hands, then blowing into his web of palms, and Jaya and Kartik trail him.

Jayesh- Dear friends, I have an announcement to make: Jaya and Kartik have decided to retreat the next morning. So, let's cheer for them for making it here.

Noises of mourning prevail, and the bonfire seems to simmer. A pinch of joy on Jaya's face and remorse on Kartik's broadcast of the unsaid

Maya overhears some murmurs. "At last, the female factor wins over."

Maya (composed while adding some dry shoots to the fire to revive it) Comrades, now that we will be a pack of 10 for the next day's excursion, let's have a gala time this evening. Let me share a story that my grandmother often recited to me when I was a kid.

Once upon a time, there was an island where all the feelings lived together. One day, there was a storm in the sea, and the island was about to get drowned. All the feelings were scared, but love made a boat to escape. Every feeling boarded the boat, and only one feeling was left. So, love got down to see who it was. It was ego. Love tried and tried, but ego (as ego is) refused to vacate the island. Meanwhile, the water was rising too. Every feeling asked love to leave ego and come into the boat. But love was made to love. In the end, all the feelings escape, and love dies with ego on the island.

So, what's the moral of the story?

Love dies because of ego! So, ego is the biggest destroyer of any relationship.

Pregnant silence ensues for a few moments until everyone hears a summons for dinner under the constellation of stars.

While Jaya and Kartik leave early, calling it a day, others continue with their fun and frolic. Some even chorus songs in their native language, and some in broken notes, but all the endeavors get well-received by everyone.

The next morning, everyone gathers with their bags zipped. But Jaya and Kartik are again absent. After a few moments, the duo makes an appearance. The counterparts step forward to bid their final goodbyes.

Jaya: Folks, would you mind if we both joined you for the remaining hike?

Everyone looks at each other, shell-shocked.

Jiya- Of course, we never wanted to lose you. But, if I may ask, what's the reason behind the change of heart?

Jaya: Last night, after being all ears to Maya's story, I realized that for me, it was less of a trip to the Bali Pass and more of an ego trip. During our courtship period, Kartik expressed his wish to go on the Bali Pass trek and how keen he was for me to accompany him. I agreed, not knowing how rugged it could be. After the first few kilometers, I gathered how herculean it would be. So, I started cursing myself for affirming and Kartik for dragging me in. This made the journey even more treacherous for me.

However, Maya's story was an eye-opener for me. Last night, we slept without uttering a word to each other, but I was awakened by the ego hosting in me.

This morning, when we woke up, I was astonished to see we had both switched places. Kartik was hellbent on a U-turn, and I was resuming our trek. I knew that despite his resistance, his heart was all in for the incline, not the decline. So, here we are, geared up to make it to our destination.

Once again, Maya receives a round of applause from the bystanders. After Maya and Jaya exchange a wink, the team sets off for the march.

In the next 4 hours, they reached Devsu Thach and head for Ruinsara Tal as their destination for the day.

Jiya- You are a magician, Maya. I admire your approach to contending with tough terrain. Now I can fathom out that the main reason for discord in my life is because of my ego. I think I need to revamp myself and my relationships. You have made me rethink my decision to seek a divorce. I can now recall numerous incidents where a clash with my husband and in-laws could have been surpassed had I not hoarded my ego.

Maya- I thank you for your appreciative words, and I appreciate you reconsidering your verdict. It is not that a divorce is bad, as society deems it. Sometimes, this could be a favorable decision. Last year, I met a college friend after many years. Rather, we had not met for the last decade. So, one day, when I was on an official tour in her city, we connected and planned to meet after my seminar.

When she arrived, she was smiling as always, but her swollen eyes relayed a different story. Upon insisting, she revealed that her husband was a drunkard and abused her physically. To add insult to injury, her in-laws slammed her for the girl child. She had a seven-year-old daughter. Besides, my friend's parents also blamed her for all the misery. She said that she had tried her teeth and nails to set things right, but to no avail.

After hearing her, I deciphered that her husband would not change and her in-laws would not stop taunting her. So, I asked her to opt for a divorce. Initially, she was apprehensive about the same dogma: 'what would others say', 'As I am a housewife, I cannot even get a job', 'how will I raise my daughter', etc., etc.

Then I told her a story about self-dignity.

Be Self-Dignified

A speaker started his seminar by showing a biscuit of gold to the public. He asked the people, "Who wants this?" It was no surprise to see that all of them raised their hands. He offered to give that biscuit to one of them. But he insisted that he would do something about it. The speaker dropped it from the dice, showed it again to the crowd, and repeated the question. Still, everyone raised their hands. He then put the gold biscuit on the ground and stepped on it. Again, he raised it and offered it to the public.

The people gathered there still showed interest in taking that pricey biscuit, despite seeing how dirty the metal was.

Then the speaker said, "No matter what I did to this gold bar, you all still wanted it. You all went in favor of my offer just because of the value it holds. This value never depreciated, despite what I did to it.

Similarly, value yourself despite the painful conditions or failures. Believe in yourself and work hard to achieve success. Do not degrade yourself just because of the temporary setbacks."

We are all unique and gifted with some talent. Therefore, we must use these gifts as our strength to build our identity, even if that invites the wrath of people around us.

I said to my friend that she should come out of the cobweb of her helplessness, as it was not helping her anymore. Moreover, her daughter, too, could have developed the same attitude of surrendering to challenges.

In the same week, she filed for divorce and also got custody of her daughter. She did not ask for even a single penny in alimony. I helped her get a loan from a bank, and she opened a boutique by the name of "The Stitch of Life."

Last week, when I called her, she said that she had settled most of the loan and that her daughter was going to a convent school. Her voice spoke volumes about the freedom and gratification she was cherishing.

At the same time, I advocate that separation should be the last alternative. In my friend's case, her life would have deteriorated further had she continued her marriage.

Hear Before Being Heard

Once upon a time, there was a wise old man who lived in a small village. He was known for his wisdom and good advice, and people from all around would come to him seeking guidance.

One day, a young man came to the wise old man and said, "I have a problem. I feel like no one listens to me, and I don't know what to do."

The wise old man smiled and said, "I have a piece of advice for you. Before you speak, make sure you listen carefully to what others are saying."

The young man was confused and asked, "But how will that help me?"

The wise old man replied, "When you listen carefully to what others are saying, you will understand their perspective and their needs. You will be able to respond in a way that shows that you value their opinion, and they will be more likely to listen to you in return."

The young man took the wise old man's advice to heart and started to practice listening carefully before speaking. He found that people started to listen to him more, and he was able to communicate more effectively.

Over time, the young man became known for his excellent communication skills and his ability to listen carefully to others. He became a respected leader in his community and was able to achieve his goals by understanding the needs and perspectives of others.

The wise old man's advice taught the young man an important lesson: before speaking, it is essential to listen carefully to what others are saying. By doing so, we can understand their perspective and respond in a way that shows we value their opinion. This is the key to effective communication and building strong relationships with others.

So, whether it is with your spouse, in-laws, relatives, or friends, the creases can be ironed out with a cross-table talk. In most instances, understanding the other person's point of view before expressing your stance can make a remarkable difference.

"Hearing before being heard" means actively listening to someone before expressing your own thoughts or opinions. It's a valuable communication skill that allows for deeper understanding and more productive conversations.

When you hear someone out, you show them that you value their thoughts and opinions. You can gather more information, which can help you form a more well-rounded response. It's essential to resist the urge to interrupt or talk over someone and instead give them your full attention.

Active listening involves not only hearing the words being said but also paying attention to nonverbal cues such as body language and tone of voice. Once the other person has finished speaking, you can then respond thoughtfully and respectfully, taking into account what you have just heard.

Overall, hearing before being heard is a crucial component of effective communication, building relationships, and resolving conflicts.

Do Not Expect Conflicts Will Not Come Your Way

Conflicts are bound to happen in any relationship. So, anticipating that bones of contention will not happen makes you less prepared to handle them. Rather, be zealous to handle clashes and create a win-win situation. Here are some suggestions to handle them productively:

Communicate openly and honestly: Communication is key in any relationship. Be open and honest with your partner, and express your thoughts and feelings in a respectful and constructive way.

Practice empathy: Try to put yourself in your partner's shoes and understand their point of view. This can help you be more compassionate and avoid misunderstandings.

Respect each other's boundaries: It's important to respect your partner's boundaries and not push them beyond their comfort zone. This can prevent conflicts related to personal space, privacy, and individual needs.

Find common ground: Identify areas of common interest or values and work together to build on them. This can help to strengthen your relationship and reduce conflicts.

Practice forgiveness: Forgiveness is a powerful tool that can help to avoid conflicts in a relationship. Learn to let go of minor disagreements and focus on the positive aspects of your relationship.

Dealing with conflict in a relationship requires patience, understanding, and respect for your partner. By practicing effective communication, empathy, and forgiveness, you can build a strong and healthy relationship that can withstand any challenge.

Jiya- You are awesome, Maya. I have gotten carried away to the extent that I yearn to call my husband and in-laws right now and get things right. But you have talked about forgiveness. It takes a lot of wit to forgive someone. I have tried this many times but ended up blaming people and situations.

More on letting go

Maya: This reminds me of a real-life incident about forgiveness. The two characters in this anecdote are a woman named Mary Johnson and a man named Oshea Israel. In 1993, Oshea was just 16 years old when he shot and killed Mary's only son, 20-year-old Laramiun Byrd, during an argument at a party in Minneapolis.

Oshea was convicted of murder and sentenced to 25 years in prison. During his time in prison, he began to reflect on his actions and the pain he had caused. He decided to reach out to Mary Johnson, the mother of the man he had killed, and ask for forgiveness.

Mary was initially reluctant to forgive Oshea, but she eventually agreed to meet with him. They sat down face-to-face in prison, and Oshea apologized for what he had done. Mary was moved by Oshea's genuine remorse and began to see him as more than just a murderer.

Over time, Mary and Oshea developed a strong bond. Mary began visiting Oshea in prison regularly and even spoke on his behalf at his parole hearing. In 2010, after serving 17 years in prison, Oshea was released on parole.

Mary welcomed Oshea into her home, and he became like a son to her. They now travel together, sharing their story of forgiveness and encouraging others to let go of anger and resentment. They even started an organization called "From Death to Life," which promotes healing and reconciliation between victims of violent crimes and their offenders.

Mary and Oshea's story is a powerful example of the transformative power of forgiveness. Despite the horrific tragedy that occurred, they were able to find healing and build a strong bond based on forgiveness and understanding. Their story serves as an inspiration to others and reminds us that forgiveness is always possible, even in the most difficult circumstances.

Therefore, forgiveness is a powerful tool that can help promote emotional well-being and works best in improving relationships. It involves letting go of negative feelings and resentments towards someone who has wronged you. So Jiya, here are some quick tips for you:

Acknowledge your feelings: It's important to acknowledge and process your emotions before you can forgive someone. Take the time to understand how you feel and why you feel that way.

Be open to forgiveness: Forgiveness is a choice, and it's important to be open to it. You may not be ready to forgive immediately, but being open to the possibility of forgiveness can help you move in that direction.

Try to understand the other person's perspective: I repeat, empathy can be a powerful tool for forgiveness. Try to understand why the other person behaved the way they did and what factors may have influenced their behavior.

Let go of resentment: Holding onto resentment can be harmful to your emotional well-being. Practice letting go of negative feelings and focusing on the positive aspects of your life.

Express your forgiveness: If you feel ready to forgive someone, it can be helpful to express this to them directly. This can help restore trust and improve your relationship.

Seek support if needed: Forgiveness can be difficult, and it's okay to seek support from a therapist, trusted friend, or family member if you need help processing your emotions.

Remember, forgiveness is a process that takes time and effort. It's important to be patient with yourself and with the other person as you work towards forgiveness. By practicing forgiveness, you can improve your emotional well-being and strengthen your relationships.

Jiya- Thanks Maya. I will certainly try to incorporate these suggestions into my life. Let me say, you are a completely transformed person compared to the one I knew in our academic days. You are like the uncontaminated air that fills the aura with liveliness.

Maya (with a courteous smile): Ahaa, enough of flattery, Jiya. I am still in the learning mode, and I will be until my validity on this planet. Now let's get something to eat, as my intestines are grumbling.

Chapter 4

THE BLUEPRINT FOR AN EMPOWERED MINDSET

"The mind is the limit. As long as the mind can envision the fact that you can do something, you can do it, as long as you really believe 100 percent."

– Napoleon Hill

After a steep hill climb, the team crosses Devsu Bugyal, where they find themselves surrounded by lush greenery and undulating meadows. The breathtaking views of snow-capped peaks, vast valleys, and cascading waterfalls are a sight to behold. In front of them is Kala Nag (Black Peak), which is an ideal trek for the expedition.

As they hike through a narrow alley in the woods, Jayesh hushes the trekkers to freeze. Astounded, everyone gazes at the wave of fright on Jayesh's face.

Jayesh (while pointing at a spot about 20 yards away): Friends, we have got company. There is black bear behind that bush. Generally, these animals are habituated to human presence, but they may charge in if they sense danger. So, let's not bother our heavy-weight chap and stay here until we are out of the danger zone.

However, to everyone's surprise, they see a bear cub trailing the mama bear and then another gigantic papa bear.

Sows (adult female bears) and boars (adult male bears) are usually not aggressive, but if there is a baby bear in the pack, they may turn hostile.

Jiya (whisperingly): This big daddy reminds me of the huge black bear in the Rampage movie. The baby cub is cute enough to be cuddled. Is this giant couple enough to toss us down the valley?

Jayesh (in an agitated mumble): For God's sake, Jiya, can you please hold your tongue wag for some time?

Maya (self-talking with a smile): These are such gorgeous creatures, Jiya, but mighty enough to give us a death blow all at once. So, hold your bears—I mean horses, Jiya.

As seconds tick by, the crackling of the dry leaves gets louder. In the next minute, what they see is something that is going to remain in their memory for a long time, if they ever survive.

The mama bear is sitting in the middle of the pathway, sheltering the baby but alert to strike. Her knuckles were positioned on the ground like a sprinter, ready for a 100-meter race. Guarding them is the big daddy in the stance of a yeti, parading his deadly jaws and razor-sharp claws. As he roars, the cacophony of birds shoots to the sky, and the monkeys start to flee on the branches in leaps and bounds, making the scene more horrific. roar that could have created an avalanche in the nearby mountains. The echo of the roar was enough to birth a heart attack in the frail-hearted within a radius of several kilometers.

Drops on the faces are dripping from the eyes and forehead. While some start to chant prayers silently, others bid their final goodbyes to their loved ones wordlessly. However, there is one person who is also caught by the wave of terror, but her mind is constantly surfing for something.

As the bear family starts approaching the drenched 12 statues plus 2 local helpers and a guide (Jayesh), Maya inches to the front.

Jayesh- What are you doing, Maya? Stay where you are. Any movement can trigger an attack. You are risking everyone's life.

However, Maya turns a deaf ear to Jayesh, and snails take the lead. This act was enough to fan the flames in the enraged brutes merely 20 yards away. Taking this as an offense, the boar gears up to storm in.

In a fraction of a second, Maya lays down her walking stick, slowly steps back, and waves her arms above her head. In a calm voice, she intonates, "We are not here to harm you. You are so awesome and powerful. We respect you, and we are sorry to have intruded into your territory. Please let us go."

Having lost the ability to move even a finger, all 11 eyeballs stuck at Maya, trying to guess what she was up to. Some are even wondering, 'Do bears understand human language? But they are the wilds.' At this moment, even muted laughter seems to have escaped to the other side of the hill.

On the other end, the three were four-legged, looking at Maya while twisting their heads. The cub gets off her mother's lap and starts strolling toward the crew. A mellowed yet dreadful 'Oh my God' escapes everyone's lips with heavy panting. A torturous end now seems avoidable.

The mama bear bustles and slaps the baby on the hip, as if teaching a lesson to not go close to strangers. Then she tucks the cub into her belly and starts making her way down the hillside. Whereas, the papa bear still perches in the middle of the walkway. As he sees the mama bear reaching safe ground, he too follows suit.

Witnessing the bear family eloping, everyone gathers breath as if they have nosedived into the ocean without an oxygen mask.

Jaya-Bingo Maya, you have saved our lives. Now I know what a death-defying experience means. That was a close shave, and, most likely, we would have been wiped off by the brutes. But how did you do this? Were you not scared when you stepped to the forefront?

Maya (after letting off a long 'phew): Jaya, I was scared stiff, but as they say, challenges are masked opportunities, so I fixated my mind on taking the initiative. I had read about animal attacks and knew that most untamed animals, especially bears, switch to bluff charges when they encounter a human. These bluff attempts are meant to scare or intimidate us. I also learned how to deal with such a situation when it arises. But the key factor is how you respond. If you surrender to the challenge or try to prove your supremacy, you may invite an unfavorable consequence.

Everyone claps for Maya, and the chorus is not thundering to invite the trio back. With a thick film of tears, some could not believe they were alive. And the journey continues.

Jiya- Let me ask you: What is the number one factor that determines success in any domain, may it be in professional life, relationships, or overall wellbeing?

Maya- Mindology! It is the mindset you harbor that determines the quality of your life and the milestones you achieve.

"Whether you think you can or you think you can't, you're right."

– Henry Ford

Mindology

If you think you can escape the bear, you can, and vice versa. Our mindset is a collection of beliefs, attitudes, and assumptions that shape how we perceive and respond to the world around us. It influences our thoughts, feelings, and behaviors and can have a profound impact on our ability to learn, grow, and achieve our goals.

Everyone in this world operates from either of two mindsets: fixed or growth. A fixed mindset is characterized by the belief that our abilities and qualities are largely predetermined and cannot be changed. People with a fixed mindset may avoid challenges or risks, become defensive or discouraged when faced with criticism or failure, and be more likely to give up on goals or pursuits that they deem too difficult.

I always wanted to be a compelling speaker. But the fear of the stage would make my blood run cold. I would spend hours every day mirror-practicing and self-talking, dreaming of becoming a great speaker someday.

One day, my manager assigned me probably the toughest project of my life: to prepare a PowerPoint and give a presentation to our prospective clients. Apart from our premium clients, even the company MD was supposed to be a part of that presentation. Initially, I was excited about the project, but as I started to work on it, I became increasingly frustrated. The fear of facing a sizeable audience threw me off balance. Besides, a bad presentation would have put my job at stake.

The more I practiced, the more negative thoughts overpowered me. I started to believe, 'I am not good enough, and I cannot ever achieve this dream of being an impactful speaker.' I felt discouraged and defeated and decided to draft my resignation letter. I was sure that I would be asked to leave after the presentation was over. So, I was all set to give up.

It was Wednesday evening, and I had to deliver the presentation on Friday morning. I was battling with my presentation script when the doorbell rang. Frustrated, I answered the door and saw my friend Naina standing with a usual charming smile, blunt-cut hair, and tall stature. Naina and I are college friends, and we usually drop by each other's place without intimating. That was a pocket-sized relief, as I was weary of getting the ducks in a row.

Seeing me in a tizzy, she asked, "Dear Maya, why do you seem to me like a cat on a hot tin roof?" I grinned and explained my stuck-in-the-rut situation. That seemed to fire up Naina's enthusiasm. In an instant, she hurled her hanging purse aside, hopped onto the couch, rested her chin on her knuckles, and uttered, "I am your audience. Baby, now prove your mettle to me."

Bewildered, I turned my laptop 90 degrees to my eyes and started with my presentation. During the course, Naina interrupted me a couple of times and catapulted some questions, which, fortunately, I had answers to. As I wrapped up, Naina continued to look at me without batting an eyelid. After a few moments, she stood up and said, "Maya, I have been delivering presentations throughout the five years of my career as the sales head. But now I have started to envy you; I wonder if I could be as fantastic as you."

I was amazed and realized that my negative thoughts had been holding me back. And Naina's words were confirmed when I received a standing ovation after my presentation and an email confirming a promotion the next week.

From that moment on, I decided to change my mindset. Instead of thinking about my limitations, I started to focus on my strengths. I practiced every day, and last week I received an invitation to deliver a speech at TED Talks.

I learned a valuable lesson about the power of mindset. When I stopped limiting myself and started believing in my abilities, I was able to achieve great things.

In contrast, a growth mindset is characterized by a belief that our abilities and qualities can be developed and improved over time through effort, practice, and learning. People with a growth mindset tend to embrace challenges and see failure as an opportunity for growth and learning. They are more likely to persist in the face of setbacks, seek out feedback and constructive criticism, and have a greater sense of resilience and optimism.

One real-life example of a growth mindset comes from the story of Michael Jordan, widely considered to be one of the greatest basketball players of all time.

When Jordan was a high school student, he was cut from his varsity basketball team. This was a huge blow to Jordan, who had always dreamed of playing basketball at the highest level.

But instead of giving up, Jordan decided to use this setback as motivation to work even harder. He spent hours practicing every day, honing his skills, and improving his game. He also started playing on his junior varsity team, where he was able to get more playing time and develop his skills.

By the time he graduated from high school, Jordan had become one of the best players in the state. He went on to play college basketball at the University of North Carolina, where he won a national championship and was named the NCAA Player of the Year.

Jordan later received a draft pick from the Chicago Bulls, where he went on to have one of the most successful NBA (National Basketball Association) careers. He won six NBA championships, five MVP (Most Valuable Player) awards, and was named an All-Star 14 times.

Throughout his career, Jordan embodied a growth mindset. He was never satisfied with his performance and was always looking for ways to improve. He famously said, "I've missed more than 9,000 shots in my career. I've lost almost 300 games. Twenty-six times, I've been trusted to take the game-winning shot and missed. I've failed over and over and over again in my life. And that is why I succeed."

Jordan's story is a powerful example of how a growth mindset can lead to incredible success. By approaching setbacks as opportunities to learn and grow, we can achieve great things and reach our full potential.

Another example is that of Sara Blakely, the founder of the shapewear company Spanx.

Blakely started her career as a salesperson for a fax machine company, but she always knew she wanted to be an entrepreneur. She had an idea for a better kind of shapewear, but she had no experience in fashion or design.

Despite her lack of experience, Blakely decided to pursue her idea. She spent two years researching and developing her product, often working long hours and funding the project with her own savings.

When she finally launched Spanx, she faced numerous setbacks and challenges. Stores were hesitant to stock her product, and she struggled to get her brand off the ground.

But Blakely refused to give up. She approached every challenge with a growth mindset, viewing each setback as an opportunity to learn and improve. She worked tirelessly to promote her product, and she was eventually able to secure a deal with Neiman Marcus, a major department store chain.

From there, Spanx took off, becoming one of the most successful shapewear brands in the world. Today, the company is valued at over $1 billion, and Blakely is a billionaire herself.

Throughout her journey, Blakely has embodied a growth mindset. She has always been willing to take risks, learn from her mistakes, and keep pushing forward. As she once said, "I think failure is nothing more than life's way of nudging you that you are off course. My attitude toward failure is not attached to the outcome but to not trying. It is liberating."

Blakely's story is a powerful reminder that anyone can achieve success with a growth mindset.

Working on your mindset is a continuous process that requires self-reflection, practice, and dedication. Here are some tips to help you work on your mindset:

Identify your current mindset. Take some time to reflect on your beliefs and attitudes. Are you generally optimistic or pessimistic? Do you believe that your abilities are fixed or that you can develop them through effort? Identifying your current mindset can help you understand where you need to focus your efforts.

Practice self-awareness: Take time to observe your thoughts and feelings without judgment. Observe how your body responds to different situations. When you notice negative or limiting thoughts, challenge them with more positive and empowering ones. Practice gratitude and focus on the things that are going well in your life. Reflect on your successes and failures. Consider what you learned from each experience.

Develop a growth mindset by viewing setbacks as opportunities for improvement: Analyze what went wrong and what you can do differently next time. Focus on the process of learning rather than just the outcome. Celebrate your progress and view mistakes as valuable feedback.

Surround yourself with positive influences: Seek out people who encourage and support you in your goals and aspirations. Join clubs or groups that align with your interests and passions. This is a great way to meet like-minded individuals who share your values and goals. Spend time with those who lift you up and make you feel good about yourself. Participate in activities that make you feel happy and fulfilled, such as volunteering, exercise, or hobbies. This can help you connect with positive and like-minded individuals. Seek the help of a mentor or coach who can provide guidance and support.

Take action: Practice new habits and behaviors that align with your desired mindset. For example, if you want to develop a growth mindset, set goals that challenge you and focus on the process of learning and improvement. Break down big goals into smaller, manageable tasks. This will help you avoid feeling overwhelmed and make progress toward your goals. Set timelines and deadlines to keep yourself accountable. Take consistent action towards your goals because consistency is key to making progress and achieving your goals.

Be patient: Developing a new mindset takes time and effort. Focus on the process of achieving your goals rather than just the outcome. Enjoy the journey and the learning experiences along the way. Don't expect instant results or give up if you experience setbacks. Allow yourself to take breaks and recharge when needed. This can help you avoid burnout and maintain your patience and focus. Remember that everyone makes mistakes and that they are an opportunity to learn and grow. Stay committed to the process, and celebrate your progress along the way.

Developing a growth mindset can help us overcome obstacles, learn from failures, and achieve our goals. It can also lead to greater satisfaction and fulfillment in our personal and professional lives. If you surrender to a challenge, most likely, you are heading for disaster. There's nothing wrong with failing, but not trying is, for sure, a recipe for failure. Besides, setbacks are a part of life. We should learn from our failures and move forward. As they say, there is nothing called failure; either you succeed or you learn.

Jiya- Yes, I agree that failures are the stepping stones to success. But it is backbreaking to handle failures. If you ask me about my failures, I can run off with a complete list in my mouth. However, if you ask me about my successes, I might get into a brown study, and not just me; I see many people around brooding over failures.

Maya- You are right. Unfortunately, a majority of people take failures as their inefficiency and the terror of failing. The first step is to accept that failures are an imperative part of life.

Failures are a part of life

No matter how hard we try, we will inevitably experience setbacks and make mistakes along the way. But it's important to remember that failure is not the end of the road. In fact, it can be a valuable opportunity to learn and grow.

When we experience failure, it's natural to feel discouraged and disappointed. We may feel like giving up or like we are not good enough. But it's important to remember that failure is not a reflection of our worth or our abilities. It's simply a part of the learning process.

One way to overcome failure is to adopt a growth mindset. Instead of seeing failure as a sign of defeat, we can view it as an opportunity to learn and improve. We can ask ourselves what went wrong, what we could have done differently, and how we can do better next time. By doing so, we can turn our failures into valuable lessons and use them to achieve even greater success in the future.

We may experience setbacks, but we can always pick ourselves up and keep moving forward. We can try again, learn from our mistakes, and work even harder to achieve our goals.

In the end, failures are a natural part of life. But they don't have to define us or hold us back. With a growth mindset and a determination to keep moving forward, we can turn our failures into opportunities and achieve our dreams.

Poverty, abuse, and instability were a part of Oprah Winfrey's childhood. She grew up in a rural area of Mississippi with her grandmother and faced many difficulties. Despite these obstacles, Oprah was determined to create a better life for herself.

Early in her career, Oprah experienced numerous setbacks and failures. She was fired from her first job as a television anchor in Baltimore and struggled to find work in the industry. She was told she was "unfit for TV" and that she didn't have the right look or personality.

But Oprah refused to give up. She continued to work hard and pursue her dream of becoming a successful television host. She landed a job as a talk show host in Chicago and quickly gained a loyal following. Her show, The Oprah Winfrey Show, became a national sensation, and Oprah became one of the most influential and beloved figures in American television.

Throughout her career, Oprah has been open about her struggles with failure and adversity. She has spoken about her battles with weight, her difficult childhood, and the challenges she faced as a black woman in the entertainment industry. But she has always refused to be defined by her failures. Instead, she has used them as opportunities to learn, grow, and inspire others.

Oprah's story is a powerful reminder that even in the face of adversity and failure, we can achieve great things. By staying focused on our goals, working hard, and refusing to give up, we can overcome even the toughest obstacles and achieve our dreams.

Here are some steps that can help you overcome the fear of failure:

Identify the source of your fear: Understanding the root cause of your fear of failure can help you overcome it. It could be related to past experiences, negative self-talk, or societal pressure.

Change your mindset: Instead of seeing failure as a sign of defeat, try to see it as an opportunity to learn and grow. Adopting a growth mindset can help you approach challenges with a more positive outlook.

Set realistic goals: Setting goals that are challenging yet achievable can help you build confidence and reduce your fear of failure. Break your goals down into smaller, manageable tasks to make them feel more achievable.

Embrace failure: Accept that failure is a natural part of the learning process. When you experience setbacks, take the time to reflect on what you learned and how you can do better next time.

Seek support: Surround yourself with people who will support and encourage you. Talk to friends, family, or a therapist about your fears and challenges.

Practice self-care: Taking care of yourself physically, mentally, and emotionally can help you build resilience and overcome your fear of failure. Make time for activities that you enjoy and prioritize self-care in your daily routine.

Remember, overcoming the fear of failure is a process, and it takes time and effort. Be patient with yourself, and celebrate your progress along the way. With the right mindset and support, you can overcome your fears and achieve your goals.

Chapter 5

YOU DESERVE FINANCIAL FREEDOM

"The secret to wealth is simple: Find a way to do more for others than anyone else does. Become more valuable. Do more. Give more. Be more. Serve more."

– *Tony Robbins*

As the backpackers make their way to the Ruinsara Tal, rain starts to pour in buckets, turning the rocky route into a skating rink. They come across a stream that has been bridged by two 8-foot logs, with water splashing across. As the current has gained momentum, it cannot transverse through the stream. However, crossing this connector is a task nothing less than hanging by a thread. Jayesh trailblazes and shows the team the trick of stepping through the makeshift bridge. Megha follows Jayesh and makes a safe landing, though taking a little longer to step consciously. Then a helper, Ganesha, puts his feet on the block of wood and as he reaches midway, a rolling stone hits the bridge, knocking him off balance.

Seeing Ganesha tripping off into the watercourse, everyone shrieks. Jayesh sprints to the helper, who is getting drifted by the strong current. He immediately zips off his bag, takes out a rope, and launches it into the water after a swing. "Ohhhh," everyone bawls as the end of the rope misses the target. On the third attempt, Ganesha manages to catch on to the rope. Megha darts to help Jayesh crane out the unfortunate fellow. However, the flow of the rivulet seems to gain an edge in this tug-of-war. With every attempt, Jayesh and Megha gravitate toward the stream by a few inches.

Jayesh (on top of his lungs): Dagdiya (means friend in Garhwali language). Take off that bag, go to lose some weight, and give it all you have to tear out of this creek. Come on, you are brave, dude.

Meanwhile, Maya also makes it to the other end to join Jayesh and Megha to pull them from the troubled waters. Finally, after twenty minutes of combat, Ganesha breathes on the ground. With his energy sunk to the lowest decibel and dripping clothes, he drops to the ground like a beheaded warrior. While Jayesh boosts his morale, Megha and Maya offer him towels and a water bottle to regain strength.

The heavy pour has ceased, and the remaining team members also crawl their way through the logs, now full of fraught

Jayesh- The bag that Ganesha had to let go in the stream had a day or two of our food supplies. I think we have to terminate this trek at the Ruinsara Tal, as we do not have the ration to withstand another three days. The fee for the remaining trek will be refunded once we reach the starting point.

With a feeling of remorse and horror because of the two spine-chilling incidents of the day, the trekkers advance to their compressed destination.

As they reach the Ruinsara Tal, they are left in awe by the ethereal beauty of the lake, located at 3,500 meters above sea level. Also known as God's Lake, it is adorned at the foot of the snow-capped Mount Kalanag and Bandar Poonch. Hedged in by the meadows with alpine vegetation and rosy red rhododendrons, the Ruinsara Tal is considered sacred by the inhabitants of Har-Ki-Doon Valley. According to the legends, this is the path that the eldest Pandava brother, Yudhishtra, took while enroute to Swargarohini, the doorway to heaven.

As soon as the team sets up their camps, the first thing Maya does is take stock of the remaining supplies. After making some notes on her register and Twittering with other team members, she approaches Jayesh.

Maya-Jayesh, we have mutually decided to make it to the Bali Pass.

Jayesh: But Maya, we have the groceries to survive for no more than a few meals. So, we better keep it for our return journey.

Maya: According to my calculations, we can persist for another three days without compromising much.

We have 4 kg of flour. With 1 kg of dough, we can bake 30 chapatis (Indian flatbread), which is enough to serve a one-time meal to a group of 15. This means we have flour for two days.

Another 4 kg of rice is enough to be savored with chapatis.

Plus, we have dry grains and veggies to complement the meals.

In a nutshell, the third day is our challenge for now. We mainly need a good diet before starting our trek and during the journey. So, as our dinner diet, we can feed mainly on supper and salad. This can leave us with an ample supply for the third day.

Also, I am carrying some dry fruits, nuts, and chocolates in my reserve.

The only thing we need most is H2O. We have natural springs to refill our bottles and keep progressing. So, we do not think it will be much of a hardship.

Jayesh, most of us have been enthused for months to trek to the Bali Pass, and some even for years. So, we do not want to retrace without walking the ridge of our dreams.

Jayesh (after a brief pause) I must applaud the commitment of each team member. I have never come across a group this zealous. Normally, people surrender to austerities and retire back to their comfort zones. But you guys seem to be iron-willed. Okay, let's jack up for the Bali Pass Base Camp tomorrow morning.

Megha- Thank you, Jayesh, for your encouraging words. We believe Maya is the wind beneath our wings who keeps us pushing to take another step and then another. She has been a key player on our team. And now we can declare that we are all going to rock to the Bali Pass.

A blaring hip-hip-hooray follows.

As there are two hours to go for dinner, the hikers plan to sit by the lake and soak in the evening sun.

The colors in the sky are like a brush on an artist's canvas, destined to create a marvelous work of art. The orange-gold stretched far and wide. But this is just a prelude to the next dawn of more determination and endurance.

Shreya (another team member) Maya, I admire you for fine-tooth-combing the stock and computing even the microscopic details. As they say, where there is a will, there is a way. So, you have found the way to our destination. Even I carried some stuff for an emergency, which I gobbled on the very first day as those were mostly chocolates. The same happens in the case of my finances. I tend to fritter away most of my salary in the first week.

Rayan: Well, managing my finances is the area where I grapple the most. I often ask myself, 'Where is all my money?' I think I am working just to pay my bills and EMIs. I wish I would have been born with a silver spoon so that I would not have to worry about my financial health.

Jiya- Fortunately, I have not faced any financial crises so far because my husband has several businesses to keep us well-heeled. But he often asks me to learn about financial planning. I have joined several workshops only to learn about some canned solutions, and most of them have become obsolete.

Maya- First of all, let us understand what financial planning is.

Financial planning is the process of creating a comprehensive strategy to manage your finances to achieve specific financial goals. This process involves assessing your current financial status, identifying financial objectives, creating a plan to achieve those objectives, and regularly reviewing and adjusting the plan as necessary.

It covers a wide range of financial activities, including budgeting, saving, investing, retirement planning, tax planning, insurance planning, and estate planning. The goal of financial planning is to maximize financial resources and achieve long-term financial objectives, such as buying a home, funding education, saving for retirement, or starting a business.

Now, let us walk through the 'why'.

Why is financial planning pivotal?

After completing my academics, I landed my first job. Excited about her new found financial independence, I started to spend freely on things I had always wanted but couldn't afford before.

I signed up for multiple credit cards and started using them to pay for everything from clothes and shoes to night out with friends. At that time, I did not pay much attention to my spending or my credit card balances, and before I knew it, I had accumulated a fat bill in debt.

As my debt grew, I started to feel overwhelmed and stressed. I struggled to make my minimum payments each month, and the interest charges continued to accrue. Also, my credit score and my ability to get approved for loans or credit in the future became a matter of worry for me.

Realizing that I needed to take control of my finances, I sought the help of a financial advisor. Together, we developed a plan to help me pay down my debt and improve my credit score. We also worked on developing better financial habits, such as budgeting and saving.

Over time, I was able to pay off my debt and get my finances back on track. However, I learned a valuable lesson about the dangers of financial mismanagement and the importance of being mindful of my spending and my debt. I set in stone that I would take the reins of finances into my own hands.

Therefore, I started reading numerous books and watching videos by experts to stay updated.

Following is what I have gathered so far. Financial planning is instrumental for:

Achieving Financial Goals: Financial planning helps us define our financial goals, both short-term and long-term, and develop a roadmap to achieve those goals. This can include saving for a down payment on a home, funding retirement, paying for education, or starting a business.

Budgeting: It allows us to create and maintain a budget, which aids in tracking expenses, reducing debt, and saving money. A budget can help ensure that expenses are kept in check and that we do not overspend.

Risk Management: Financial planning helps us manage financial risks, such as unexpected expenses, loss of income, or market fluctuations. This can include strategies such as insurance, emergency funds, and diversification of investments.

Tax Planning: With a plan in place, we can optimize our tax situation by taking advantage of tax breaks and deductions and avoiding unnecessary taxes.

Estate Planning: Financial planning can help us plan for the transfer of assets in the event of death and minimize estate taxes and other expenses.

There are many stories of people who have gone from rags to riches, but there are also stories of people who have gone from riches to rags. You might have heard about Mike Tyson, the former heavyweight boxing champion.

Rayan: Indeed, he is someone I follow. He is a legendary boxer.

Maya: When his career was in full bloom, Tyson was one of the wealthiest athletes in the world. He earned over $300 million in prize money and endorsements, and he spent his money on extravagant cars, homes, and parties. However, his spending habits were not sustainable, and he soon found himself in financial trouble.

In 2003, Tyson filed for bankruptcy, owing over $27 million to creditors. He had spent his money on a lavish lifestyle, and he had also made poor financial decisions, such as buying a tiger as a pet and purchasing a fleet of expensive cars. He had also faced legal troubles, including a prison sentence for rape, which had cost him millions in legal fees.

After his bankruptcy, Tyson had to sell off many of his assets, including his homes and cars, to pay off his debts. He also had to make a career comeback, returning to boxing and other ventures to earn money. Today, he is estimated to have a net worth of around $3 million, a fraction of what he once had.

The story of Mike Tyson is a cautionary tale about the dangers of overspending and making poor financial decisions.

It also highlights the importance of financial planning, even for those who have a lot of money. Without a solid financial plan and a commitment to responsible spending, even the wealthiest individuals can find themselves in financial trouble.

In 1988, William "Bud" Post won the Pennsylvania Lottery jackpot worth $16.2 million. At the time, he was living on disability payments and was in a difficult financial situation. He immediately quit his job and began living a lavish lifestyle, spending money on cars, boats, and vacations.

However, Post soon found himself in financial trouble. Family members and friends had swindled him out of a large portion of his money, and he had also made poor investments and spent extravagantly. He was sued multiple times, and he eventually filed for bankruptcy in 1996, only 8 years after winning the lottery.

After filing for bankruptcy, Post's life continued to spiral out of control. He was in and out of jail for various offenses, and he suffered from health problems and addiction. In 2006, he died at the age of 66, nearly penniless and with a legacy of financial mismanagement.

Sachin Tendulkar and Vinod Kambli, once cricketing partners, have experienced contrasting financial trajectories. Tendulkar's astute financial decisions and diversified ventures have secured his wealth. As of my latest update in Oct 2023, his net worth was estimated at around $170 million. Beyond cricket, he invested in businesses like Smaaash Entertainment and also owned properties in Mumbai.

In contrast, Kambli faced financial challenges. His net worth significantly dwindled compared to his cricketing days due to less consistent earnings and investments. Reports suggested Kambli's net worth was around $100,000, considerably lower than Tendulkar's. His limited post-cricket career and unsuccessful attempts at various endeavors impacted his finances negatively.

Kambli, talking to Mid-Day, revealed that he is running out of money and desperately needs work to sustain his family. He admitted that his only source of income is the 30,000-rupee pension from the BCCI.

Tendulkar's shrewd choices extended beyond cricket, maintaining a prosperous lifestyle. Meanwhile, Kambli's financial choices and career diversification were less fruitful. This comparison emphasizes the importance of financial planning and post-career ventures. Tendulkar's story serves as an example of successful financial management, while Kambli's challenges highlight the complexities faced by athletes transitioning from the spotlight. Keep in mind that these figures might have changed since my last update. Top of Form

The Gift of Oseola McCarty

In a small, unassuming house in Hattiesburg, Mississippi, Oseola McCarty worked tirelessly over her ironing board. The rhythmic hum of her washing machine played the soundtrack to most of her life. For over seventy-five years, Oseola washed and ironed other people's clothes, earning modest sums that many would dismiss as mere pocket change. But Oseola had a secret. She was a saver.

Every week, she put away whatever little she could into a savings account. Her life was one of frugality and dedication.

She never married, had no children, and lived simply, without the trappings of modern luxuries like a car or even an air conditioner. For Oseola, every penny counted, and she counted every penny.

Rumors floated around town about her mysterious savings, but no one could have guessed the depth of her commitment. As years turned into decades, her small savings turned into a significant sum.

Then, in the twilight of her life, Oseola made an announcement that shocked her community: she would donate $150,000, nearly all of her life savings, to the University of Southern Mississippi to fund scholarships for needy students, particularly African-Americans.

The news spread like wildfire, and Oseola became a national sensation. Here was a washerwoman with an education that ended in the sixth grade, giving nearly everything she had, to ensure that others could pursue their dreams of higher education.

Oseola's gift was more than just money; it was a testament to the power of perseverance, the value of hard work, and the belief that we all have a role to play in lifting up the next generation. Her generosity inspired others, and donations poured into the university from all corners of the country, multiplying the effect of her gift.

Oseola McCarty passed away in 1999, but her legacy lives on. Every year, students at the University of Southern Mississippi receive scholarships bearing her name, a constant reminder of the washerwoman with a heart of gold.

In a world chasing after the next big thing, Oseola's story stands as a beacon, reminding us that greatness can be found in the most unlikely of places and that the true measure of wealth is not in what we keep but in what we give away.

Amitabh Bachchan: Rise, Fall, and Resurrection

Amitabh Bachchan, often referred to as the 'Shahenshah' (emperor) of Bollywood, is an iconic figure in the Indian film industry. With a career spanning over five decades, his journey has been filled with highs and lows, teaching lessons on perseverance and determination.

In the late 1960s and throughout the 70s and 80s, Amitabh Bachchan emerged as the 'angry young man' of Bollywood. His tall frame, baritone voice, and intense acting style in movies like 'Sholay', 'Deewar', and 'Zanjeer' resonated with the masses, making him a megastar. At his peak, it seemed like nothing could go wrong for Amitabh.

However, in the 1990s, Amitabh's film career began to decline. Concurrently, he made a daring move by launching his entertainment company, Amitabh Bachchan Corporation Ltd. (ABCL). While ABCL had a grand vision, it faced multiple challenges. It ventured into film production, distribution, and events but soon ran into financial troubles.

The company's ambitious projects, like the Miss World pageant in Bangalore in 1996, became financial burdens. Alongside, some movies produced under its banner failed to perform well at the box office. By the late 1990s, ABCL was drowning in debt, leading Amitabh to face bankruptcy. Lawsuits and legal issues plagued the star, and it seemed like the end of an era for him.

However, Amitabh, true to his on-screen persona, was not one to back down from a challenge. In the early 2000s, he made a strategic move to television, which proved to be a game-changer. He took on the role of host for the Indian version of 'Who Wants to Be a Millionaire?' titled 'Kaun Banega Crorepati' (KBC)'. The show was a massive hit, reviving Amitabh's popularity and reputation. KBC showcased Amitabh's charisma and intelligence, creating a renewed sense of respect for him among audiences of all ages.

With the renewed popularity of television, Amitabh's film career saw a resurgence. He began taking on roles that suited his age and stature, proving his versatility as an actor. Films like 'Kabhi Khushi Kabhie Gham', 'Black', 'Paa', and 'Piku' were all critically acclaimed and commercially successful.

Throughout this challenging phase, Amitabh showcased resilience, adaptability, and a never-give-up attitude. He managed to pay off all of ABCL's debts, rebrand the company, and make it profitable again.

Today, Amitabh Bachchan remains a force to be reckoned with in the entertainment industry. His story from going broke to bouncing back is a testament to his indomitable spirit and dedication, reminding us that it's never too late for a second act in life.

Winning a large sum of money can be a life-changing experience, but it requires careful planning and management to ensure that the money is used wisely and sustainably.

Therefore, failing to plan means planning to fail. Financial planning equips us for unexpected events and to make informed financial decisions. By planning ahead and being mindful of their finances, we can improve their financial well-being and achieve greater financial security.

Chapter 6

THE BLUEPRINT OF YOUR FINANCIAL PLAN

"Financial peace isn't the acquisition of stuff. It's learning to live on less than you make, so you can give money back and have money to invest. You can't win until you do this."

– Dave Ramsey

Shreya- These stories are quite astonishing. I have heard a boatload of success tales from rags to riches, but the ones you have shared are an eye-opener. If such filthy rich people can turn moneyless, we are too puny. So, what are your suggestions for secure financial planning?

Maya- Yes, a small hole sunk even the Titanic. Therefore, we should build adequate safety nets.

The first step is to gain financial education. As they say, awareness is the first step to change. We must endeavor to become financially literate by keeping the parachute of our learning open.

Financial planning can be a complex process, but here are 9 steps that can assist you in creating a robust financial plan:

1. Define your financial goals
2. Evaluate your current financial situation
3. Create and budget
4. Set up an emergency fund
5. Develop a debt management plan
6. Create an investment plan
7. Plan for retirement
8. Protect yourself with insurance
9. Review and adjust your plan regularly

Here's a step-by-step guide to manage each one of these. However, before moving on the how's, let us first learn about the why's.

1. **Define your financial goals**

   Clarity and Specificity: Your goals should be crystal clear and specific. Rather than a vague goal like "save money," specify an amount and a purpose, such as "save $10,000 for a down payment on a house." This clarity helps you stay focused and motivated.

   SMART Criteria: Utilize the SMART criteria when setting your goals – Specific, Measurable, Achievable, Relevant, and Time-bound. This framework ensures your goals are realistic and have a clear deadline, enhancing your commitment to achieving them.

   Short-Term and Long-Term Balance: Create a mix of short-term and long-term goals. While saving for a vacation might be a short-term goal, saving for retirement is a long-term one. Balancing these goals ensures you experience both immediate and enduring financial rewards.

Prioritization and Hierarchy: Not all goals are equal in importance. Prioritize your goals based on their significance and urgency. This hierarchy will help you allocate resources efficiently and tackle the most critical goals first.

Regular Review and Adaptation: Your goals aren't set in stone. Life circumstances change, and so can your goals. Regularly review your goals, adjusting them as needed to reflect changes in your life, financial situation, and aspirations.

Remember, your financial goals serve as your roadmap to success. They provide direction, motivation, and a sense of accomplishment as you work toward achieving each milestone.

2. **Evaluate your current financial situation**

   Net Worth Calculation: Calculate your net worth by subtracting your liabilities (debts) from your assets. This gives you a snapshot of your overall financial health and shows whether you're building wealth or carrying excessive debt.

   Detailed Expense Tracking: Review your spending over the past few months. Use tools like bank statements and budgeting apps to analyze where your money is going. This helps identify areas for potential savings and reveals spending patterns you might not have been aware of.

Debt-to-Income Ratio: Calculate your debt-to-income ratio by dividing your monthly debt payments by your monthly income. This ratio indicates your ability to manage your existing debts in relation to your income and guides whether you can take on additional financial commitments.

Emergency Fund Adequacy: Evaluate the size of your emergency fund. If it can cover three to six months of living expenses, you're better prepared for unexpected events. If not, consider increasing contributions to bolster your financial safety net.

Investment and Savings Review: Assess the performance of your investments and savings accounts. Are they aligned with your goals and risk tolerance? Adjustments might be necessary to optimize returns and align with your evolving objectives.

Evaluating your financial situation provides insights into your strengths and areas for improvement. It empowers you to make informed decisions, set realistic goals, and create a tailored financial plan that fits your unique circumstances.

3. **Create a budget**

Prioritization of Needs and Wants: A budget helps you distinguish between needs and wants. By categorizing your expenses, you'll see where your money is going and can make conscious decisions to prioritize essential expenses over discretionary ones.

Zero-Based Budgeting: Zero-based budgeting allocates every dollar of your income to a specific category. This ensures that your income minus expenses equals zero, leaving no room for overspending. It's a proactive approach to control your financial outcomes.

Savings and Investments Inclusion: A well-rounded budget allocates funds for savings and investments. Pay yourself first by setting aside a portion of your income for future goals, such as an emergency fund, retirement, or major purchases.

Adjustments for Flexibility: Life is dynamic, so your budget should be flexible too. Account for irregular expenses like vacations, holidays, and vehicle maintenance. Including these "sinking funds" prevents sudden financial strain when these expenses arise.

Regular Monitoring and Adjustments: Budgeting isn't a one-time task; it requires ongoing monitoring. Regularly review your budget to track your spending against your plan. Adjust as needed to stay aligned with your financial goals and accommodate any changes in your circumstances.

Creating a budget empowers you to take control of your financial journey. It guides your spending choices, helps you save for the future, and provides a roadmap to achieve your goals while living within your means.

4. **Setting up an emergency fund**

Three to Six Months of Expenses: Financial experts recommend saving three to six months' worth of living expenses in your emergency fund. This cushion provides a safety net in case of unexpected job loss, medical expenses, or other emergencies.

Separate Savings Account: Keep your emergency fund in a separate savings account from your regular checking account. This separation helps prevent the temptation of using the funds for non-emergencies.

Automatic Contributions: Set up automatic transfers from your paycheck or main account to your emergency fund. Treating this as a regular expense ensures consistent contributions without requiring conscious effort.

Replace After Use: If you use funds from your emergency fund, make replenishing it a priority. As soon as your financial situation stabilizes, allocate funds to rebuild the emergency fund to its target balance.

Adjust for Life Changes: Life circumstances change, and so should your emergency fund. Major life events like getting married, having children, or changing jobs can impact your financial needs. Regularly reassess and adjust your emergency fund based on your current situation.

An emergency fund provides peace of mind and financial stability during unforeseen challenges. It's your safety net, helping you avoid accumulating debt when unexpected expenses arise.

5. **Developing a debt management plan**

   Strategic Debt Repayment: A debt management plan helps you tackle your debts strategically. By prioritizing high-interest debts first, you can save money on interest payments over time, allowing you to pay off your debts more efficiently.

   Snowball vs. Avalanche: There are different approaches to debt repayment. The snowball method involves paying off the smallest debts first for psychological motivation, while the avalanche method focuses on debts with the highest interest rates for maximum financial savings. Choosing the right approach depends on your preferences and financial situation.

   Consolidation Options: If you have multiple debts, consolidating them into a single loan or balance transfer credit card with a lower interest rate can simplify payments and potentially reduce your overall interest costs.

   Negotiation Possibilities: In some cases, you may be able to negotiate with creditors for lower interest rates or modified payment plans. This can alleviate the financial burden and help you repay your debts more effectively.

   Long-Term Financial Freedom: Successfully implementing a debt management plan not only helps you become debt-free but also sets you on a path to long-term financial freedom. It improves your credit score, reduces financial stress, and enables you to allocate more resources towards savings and investments.

Developing a debt management plan requires discipline and commitment, but the results can be highly rewarding. It's important to tailor your plan to your unique financial circumstances and regularly review and adjust it as needed.

6. **Creating an investment plan**

Diversification is Key: A well-diversified portfolio spreads risk across various asset classes, such as stocks, bonds, and real estate. This helps mitigate the impact of a single investment's poor performance on your overall portfolio.

Investment Horizon Matters: Your investment horizon, or the time you plan to hold investments, influences your risk tolerance. Longer horizons allow for more aggressive strategies, while shorter horizons may require more conservative approaches.

Risk Tolerance Assessment: Determine your risk tolerance by evaluating how comfortable you are with market fluctuations. This assessment helps align your investments with your emotional and financial comfort levels.

Regular Rebalancing: Over time, investments may grow at different rates, causing your portfolio's allocation to shift. Regularly rebalancing—selling over-performing assets and buying under-performing ones—restores your desired asset allocation.

Consistency Trumps Timing: Timing the market is challenging and often unsuccessful. Instead, focus on consistent contributions to your investments, taking advantage of dollar-cost averaging—a strategy where you invest a fixed amount at regular intervals regardless of market fluctuations.

Remember, an investment plan should reflect your financial goals, risk tolerance, and investment horizon. Regularly review and adjust your plan to ensure it remains aligned with your evolving needs and the changing market landscape.

7. **Planning for retirement**

Start Early, Benefit More: The power of compounding works in your favor the earlier you start saving for retirement. Even small contributions can grow substantially over time, allowing you to potentially accumulate a larger retirement fund.

Estimate Retirement Expenses: Calculating your anticipated retirement expenses is essential. Consider factors like healthcare costs, living expenses, and potential travel or leisure activities to determine how much you will need to save for a comfortable retirement.

Maximize Retirement Accounts: In India, employees can benefit from retirement savings through the Employees' Provident Fund (EPF) and the National Pension System (NPS). To maximize your retirement savings, consider EPF Contributions, NPS Contributions, Atal Pension Yojana (APY),

Public and Private Provident Funds. By maximizing your contributions to these retirement-oriented schemes in India, you can take advantage of tax benefits and employer contributions, like how contributing to 401(k)s and IRAs can provide financial advantages in the United States.

Consider Social Security Strategically: Deciding when to start receiving Social Security benefits can impact your retirement income. Delaying benefits can result in higher monthly payments, while starting early may provide a longer payout period.

Account for Inflation: Inflation erodes purchasing power over time. When planning for retirement, factor in the potential impact of inflation on your expenses to ensure your savings will still meet your needs in the future.

Retirement planning requires careful consideration of various factors, and your plan should be flexible to adapt to changing circumstances. Regularly revisit your retirement plan to ensure it remains aligned with your goals and financial situation.

8. **Protecting yourself with insurance**

Diverse Insurance Options: India offers a wide range of insurance options beyond the basics like life and health insurance. You can also explore policies for motor insurance, home insurance, travel insurance, and even specialized coverage like cyber insurance.

Health Insurance is Vital: With rising healthcare costs, having comprehensive health insurance is crucial. Look for policies that cover hospitalization, pre-existing conditions, and offer cashless hospitalization services.

Term Life Insurance for Financial Security: Term life insurance provides a cost-effective way to ensure your family's financial stability in case of your unfortunate demise. Consider a policy that covers your family's needs, including education expenses and outstanding debts.

Two-Wheeler and Four-Wheeler Insurance: Motor insurance is mandatory in India, but it also protects you financially in case of accidents, damage, or theft. Explore third-party liability coverage as well as comprehensive policies for added protection.

Personal Accident Insurance: Personal accident insurance offers coverage against accidental injuries and disabilities. It can provide financial support if you're unable to work due to an accident, covering medical expenses and providing a lump sum in case of permanent disability.

When choosing insurance policies in India, carefully read the terms, coverage limits, and exclusions. Consider consulting with insurance professionals to ensure you're adequately protected against potential risks. Regularly review your insurance coverage to accommodate changes in your life or financial situation.

9. **Reviewing and adjusting your financial plan**

Changing Life Circumstances: Life is dynamic, and your financial situation evolves over time. Marriage, starting a family, changing jobs, or unexpected events can impact your plan. Regular reviews help you adapt your plan to these changes.

Market Volatility: Financial markets can be unpredictable. Regular reviews allow you to rebalance your investment portfolio based on market performance, ensuring your investments align with your risk tolerance and goals.

Inflation Impact: Inflation erodes purchasing power over time. By regularly assessing your plan, you can ensure that your savings and investments are growing at a pace that beats inflation, preserving your financial security.

New Opportunities and Goals: As you progress, new opportunities and goals may arise. Regular reviews enable you to incorporate these aspirations into your financial plan, allowing you to pursue them without compromising existing objectives.

Optimizing Tax Strategies: Tax laws change, and your financial plan should adapt to leverage available tax benefits. By reviewing your plan, you can identify opportunities to minimize tax liabilities and maximize your savings.

Remember that reviewing your financial plan should not be a one-time event. Aim to conduct comprehensive reviews at least annually, or when significant life events occur. Regular adjustments keep your plan aligned with your current circumstances and pave the way for a successful financial journey.

Financial planning requires discipline, commitment, and careful monitoring. By following the above steps, you can create a rock-hard financial plan that helps you achieve your goals and build a stable financial future.

Jiya (after a brief spell of silence)- This is again fabulous, Maya. You are a spring of wisdom. We thank you for sharing this remarkable knowledge. Now we know the 9 steps to unleash our financial freedom. It is unfortunate that financial education is so critical, yet it is not taught in our academics. No wonder why most of us remain mediocre even after decades of struggle. These steps may not be easy to follow, but gradually we can make it to unlocking our financial freedom, just like we are going to land our feet on the great Bali Pass.

Maya- Yes, you are right, Jiya. All it takes is the first step. This reminds me of our tonight's commitment to feat on salad and supper.

And everyone raises their hands in affirmation.

Chapter 7

THE CONCLUSIVE WEALTH PLAN

"Ordinary riches can be stolen; real riches cannot. In your soul are infinitely precious things that cannot be taken from you."

– *Oscar Wilde*

The next morning, Jiya wakes up at 3:30 a.m. But to her surprise, she finds Maya missing. Both have been sharing the tent since day 1 of the trek. So, she worms out of the cabin to find Maya. After treading a few steps through the tranquil periphery and darkness before dawn, she catches sight of Maya sitting beside the lake in a lotus posture.

Reaching her, Jiya taps on Maya's shoulder, which goes unnoticed. On the third tap, Maya opens her eyes as if awakened from a jolt.

Jiya: Hey, what have you been doing here? When did you wake up?

Maya (smiling after a long inhale and exhale): I begin my day by waking up at 3 a.m. and practicing meditation. This day, I chose to meditate beside this beautiful lake, for which I had been yearning for years.

There is folklore about this glacial lake, and the people of this valley consider it sacred. While meditating here, I felt celestial energies orbiting around me. I found myself in the nothingness of space, with vibrant energies dancing around. Then I heard someone calling my name and jerking my shoulder. As the voice got louder, I opened my eyes and saw you beside me.

Well, what made you rise and shine so early? We are scheduled to leave by 8 a.m., aren't we?

Jiya (looking a little stunned by Jiya's words) Today, for the first time, I woke up without an alarm. Last evening, I was overwhelmed by the knowledge you shared. I felt I had been living my life stone-blind so far. So, if you allow me, can I sum it up in six points?

Maya- Sure, I am happy to see the curious Jiya. Please go ahead.

The Wealth Framework

A wealth plan is a comprehensive financial strategy that is designed to help you build and preserve wealth over the long term. It involves a range of financial frameworks, including investment planning, retirement planning, tax planning, estate planning, risk management, and debt management. The goal of a wealth plan is to help you achieve your financial goals and ensure that you are financially secure both now and in the future.

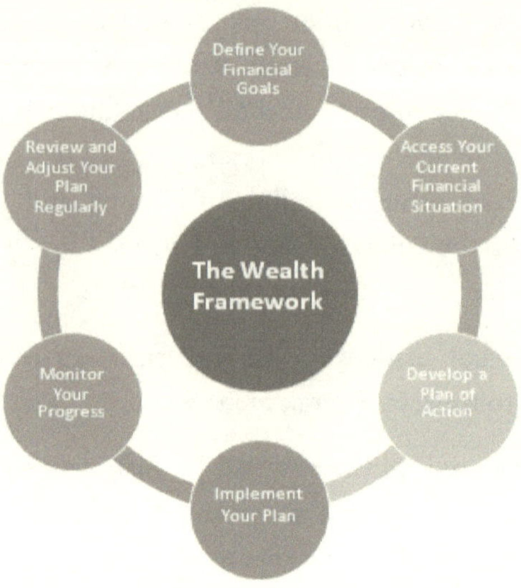

Here are some key steps to developing a wealth plan:

Establish your financial objectives: Begin by outlining your short and long-term financial objectives. Goals like purchasing a house, setting up money for retirement, paying off debt, or creating an emergency fund may fall under this category.

Evaluate your present financial position: Assess your existing financial condition, take into account your earnings, outgoings, assets, and obligations. You may use this to assess your financial situation and pinpoint opportunities for development.

Create an action plan: Create a plan of action that explains the precise measures you will take to attain your financial objectives based on your goals and financial status. This might include taking steps to increase your income, pay off debt, or invest in the stock market.

Put your plan into action: After you've created a plan of action, it's time to put it into action. To put your strategy into effect, this can include creating investment accounts, renegotiating debt, or adopting other measures.

Track your progress: Keep tabs on how you're doing in reaching your financial objectives and make any modifications. Your financial portfolio may need to be rebalanced, your spending plan may need to be modified, or your retirement plan may need to be altered.

Review and adjust your plan regularly: Last but not least, it's critical to continually assess and tweak your wealth strategy to make sure it stays in line with your objectives and financial condition. This might include altering your retirement plan, changing your tax planning, or changing your investing approach.

Conclusively, developing a wealth plan is an important step towards achieving your financial goals and ensuring long-term financial security. By defining your goals, assessing your financial situation, developing a plan of action, implementing your plan, monitoring your progress, and reviewing and adjusting your plan regularly, you can build and preserve wealth over the long term.

Maya- Bingo Jiya, you have got it all right. I am impressed by your learning.

Now, this brings us to the final pursuit. Health, relationships, wealth—all these are the vehicles that take us to our ultimate destination, contentment. But even after doing well in all these domains, if you do not feel fulfilled, then it defeats the purpose.

So, what is that one piece that unravels the puzzle?

Jiya (with a tsunami wave of inquisitiveness on her face): Oh, I am curious to know.

In the interim, they get called for breakfast.

Jiya- I can skip all the breakfasts of my life to know this final attribute. Please do not test my patience.

Maya (with a bright smile): Well, the answer is ***spirituality,*** but before scuba-diving into this, let's pamper our bellies.

Saying so, Maya gets up, and the anxious Jiya follows.

Chapter 8

SPIRITUALITY: NOT THE ULTIMATE DESTINATION, BUT THE WAY OF LIFE

"All the powers in the universe are already ours. It is we who have put our hands before our eyes and cry that it is dark."

– Swami Vivekananda

After appeasing their palates, the 12 seekers forge ahead to their destination for the day: the Bali Pass Base Camp. The queue footslogs through the heaven-driven snow. The sun is playing hide and seek amidst the clouds, which seem to have descended to the hills. The peaks are rarely visible. It seems like the snow has frozen everything around, even the time. The parts of the day – morning, afternoon, and evening – are constant. What prevails is only cold and bitterly cold.

Jiya (while quickly clawing through the footsteps carved in the snow and reaching Maya) So, you were saying something about spirituality. Is this about offering prayers to God? I do this every morning and before going to bed. Does this mean I am spiritual?

Maya (beaming a smile) Most people think that once they retire or after they have all the wealth in the world, they will start practicing spirituality. The concept of spirituality has been mis-programmed in our minds since childhood, or let me say, we know only a small fraction of spirituality. Different people might define this differently, but generally, it refers to the search for meaning, purpose, and connection with something greater than ourselves. It involves exploring our innermost beliefs, values, and experiences and can include practices such as being grateful, serving humanity, meditation, prayer, or contemplation.

Most people limit this to religion or renouncing worldly pleasures. They have set a deadline that, once they are free of all the responsibilities, they will become spiritual. To them, devotion is limited to religion or seeking refuge under God's umbrella so that they can live the rest of their lives peacefully.

No, spirituality is more encyclopedic and must be a way of life instead of the last on the to-do list. Let's now learn about the seven foundations of spirituality that we can practice in our everyday lives.

The 7 Foundations of Spirituality

1. **We are all Destined for Big Purpose.**

   Most people shell out decades of their lives for their careers or businesses, retire, and then exit this world with many unfulfilled wishes. As the monitor in the hospital room beeps, they regret that their lives could have been better had they followed their hearts. They lived their entire lives for others, not even a day for themselves. With tears nosediving to the pillow, they wish they could get another chance. And suddenly, the beep turns into a teeee.

So, wake up before the graph turns into a straight line. Nose out your big purpose and cherish your life.

Reflect on Your Passions: Start by considering the things that you are most passionate about. What activities or interests do you find most fulfilling and energizing? What brings you the greatest sense of joy and satisfaction? Your passions can provide important clues to your purpose in life.

Identify Your Values: Consider the values that are most important to you, such as compassion, creativity, justice, or personal growth. How do these values align with your current life path and choices? Identifying your values can help you clarify your priorities and make decisions that are in line with your purpose.

Look for patterns: Take a step back and look for patterns in your life. What themes or experiences have consistently shown up for you over time? Do you find yourself drawn to certain types of people, activities, or situations? Identifying these patterns can help you gain insight into your purpose and direction.

Experiment and Explore: Try new things and explore different opportunities that align with your passions and values. Volunteer, take a class, or pursue a hobby that interests you. This can help you broaden your perspective and gain new experiences that can shed light on your purpose.

Seek Support: Talk to friends, family, or a mentor about your goals and aspirations. Seek out guidance and support from those who know you well and can provide constructive feedback and encouragement.

Discovering your purpose is a process that takes time and self-reflection. Be patient with yourself and stay open to new experiences and opportunities. Over time, you will gain greater clarity and insight into your purpose and how to live a fulfilling and purposeful life.

2. **Practice Mindfulness**

Mindfulness can help reduce stress and anxiety by helping you become more aware of your thoughts and emotions and allowing you to respond to them in a more balanced and calm way. It can help improve your focus and concentration by training your brain to be more present in the moment rather than constantly getting distracted by thoughts and external stimuli. Mindfulness has been shown to enhance overall well-being and happiness by helping people cultivate more positive emotions and reduce negative ones. Besides, this can improve relationships by helping you be more present and attentive with others, communicate more effectively, and respond more skillfully to interpersonal challenges.

Here are some simple steps you can follow:

Find a quiet and comfortable place where you won't be disturbed for a few minutes.

Sit in a comfortable position, either on a chair or on a cushion, on the floor, with your back straight and your feet flat on the ground.

Close your eyes and take a deep breath through your nose, filling your lungs with air. Hold for a few seconds, and then exhale slowly through your mouth, letting go of any tension in your body.

Bring your attention to your breath. Notice the sensation of the air moving in and out of your nostrils or the rise and fall of your chest or belly.

If your mind starts to wander, gently bring it back to your breath. Don't judge or criticize yourself for getting distracted; just notice where your mind went and bring it back to the present moment.

Continue to focus on your breath for a few minutes, allowing yourself to relax and let go of any thoughts or worries.

When you are ready, slowly open your eyes and take a few deep breaths before getting up and going about your day.

Mindfulness is a practice, so don't expect to be perfect at it right away. With regular practice, you will find that you are able to be more present and focused in your daily life, which can lead to greater calm and clarity.

3. **Connect with nature**

Spending time in nature has been shown to reduce stress and anxiety levels and improve overall well-being. Nature provides a peaceful and calming environment that can help us relax and feel more centered. Being in nature has also been shown to have physical health benefits, such as reducing blood pressure, improving immune function, and lowering the risk of chronic diseases. It can promote creativity and improve problem-solving skills. The natural environment can inspire new ideas and help us think outside the box. Research has shown that spending time in nature can improve cognitive function, including attention and memory.

Go for a walk or hike in a park or natural area. Take the time to observe the plants and animals around you and appreciate the beauty of the natural environment.

Practice outdoor activities, such as camping, fishing, or gardening. These activities can help you feel more connected to the natural world and provide a sense of purpose and fulfillment.

Spend time in natural water sources, such as lakes, rivers, or the ocean. Swimming, kayaking, or simply relaxing by the water can be a great way to feel more connected to the natural environment.

Take time to simply sit and observe nature. Find a quiet spot outside, (whether it be in your backyard, a local park, or a nearby trail) and simply sit and take in the sights, sounds, and smells of the natural world around you.

Learn about the natural environment through books, documentaries, or classes. This can help you develop a deeper understanding and appreciation for the natural world and inspire you to take action to protect it.

4. **Be Grateful**

Expressing gratitude has been shown to improve mental health by reducing symptoms of depression and anxiety, increasing positive emotions, and improving overall life satisfaction. Showing gratitude can strengthen relationships by improving communication, fostering feelings of connection and empathy, and increasing feelings of trust and loyalty.

Being grateful can help increase resilience by helping us focus on the positive aspects of our lives and building emotional strength to cope with challenges. Gratitude has also been linked to physical health benefits, such as better sleep, reduced blood pressure, and a stronger immune system.

Cultivating gratitude can have many positive effects on our mental and physical health, as well as our relationships with others. Taking the time to reflect on and appreciate the good things in our lives can help us feel happier, more fulfilled, and better equipped to navigate the challenges that come our way.

Keep a gratitude journal: Each day, write down a few things you are grateful for. This can help you focus on the positive aspects of your life and build a habit of gratitude.

Express gratitude to others: Take the time to thank people in your life who have had a positive impact on you. This can help strengthen relationships and foster feelings of connection and empathy.

Reflect on difficult experiences: Even difficult experiences can offer opportunities for growth and learning. Take the time to reflect on what you have gained from challenging experiences and express gratitude for the lessons learned.

Focus on the little things: Sometimes it's easy to take the little things in our lives for granted. Take the time to appreciate the little things, such as a warm cup of tea or a beautiful sunset.

Once, a balloon seller was returning home with hunched shoulders, cursing his destiny, the Almighty, and whatnot. On that day, he could barter his balloons only for a few currency notes. He was worried that his wife and children would not be able to eat stomach-full that night.

On his way, he came across a temple where his steps froze on sight. He noticed an old blind man at the entrance, chanting praises of the Lord. It looked like he was in complete euphoria and had nothing to worry about in this world. In front of this eyeless man, there was a bowl with some alms, which were much less than the notes in the pocket of the balloon man. That rang a bell.

As the balloon man peeped into the temple, he noticed an idol painted blue, holding a flute, and beaming an ageless smile. "My son, there are many people who are more unprivileged than you. The stone-blind man does not have a home, clothes to cover his body, or family to take care of him. Still, he has no regrets. Be grateful for what you have. I might fail, but karma will not."

Suddenly, the chord of the temple bell woke the balloon man from his trance. He smiled and lipped words of gratitude. Before returning home, he paused in front of the old man, took out a note from his pocket, and placed it in the bowl. Then he plucked a balloon thread from his bamboo stand and handed it over to the elderly man. The old chap flashed his charming smile, blessed the balloon man, and then continued to chorus his prayers.

By focusing on the positive aspects of our lives and expressing appreciation for the good things, we can enhance our overall sense of well-being and build stronger, more fulfilling relationships with others.

5. **Serve Humanity**

You do not have to be a millionaire to serve others. You can do it in big or small ways. Serving others can promote a sense of well-being and fulfillment, as it allows us to connect with others, make a positive impact, and give back to our communities. It can help us develop empathy and understanding for others' experiences and struggles, which can lead to stronger and more meaningful relationships. By doing so, we can inspire others to do the same, creating a ripple effect of altruism and kindness in our communities and beyond.

Volunteer in your community: Look for local organizations or charities that align with your values and interests, and offer your time and skills to help their cause. Many organizations rely on volunteers to carry out their mission, and there are often a wide variety of roles available.

Donate to a cause you care about: If you are not able to volunteer your time, consider donating money to a cause you care about. There are many reputable organizations that work to make a positive impact in areas such as health, education, and social justice.

Practice kindness: Small acts of kindness, such as holding the door open for someone or giving a compliment, can have a big impact on someone's day. Look for opportunities to practice kindness in your daily life, and encourage others to do the same.

Use your skills to help others: If you have a particular skill or expertise, consider using it to help others. For example, if you are a lawyer, you may be able to offer pro bono legal services to those in need. If you are a teacher, you may be able to offer tutoring or mentoring to students who need extra support.

Advocate for change: Use your voice and influence to advocate for positive change in your community or on a larger scale. This may involve contacting your elected officials, writing letters to the editor, or participating in peaceful protests or demonstrations.

There are many ways to serve humanity, and no act of service is too small. Look for opportunities to make a positive impact in your own way, and don't be afraid to try new things and take on new challenges.

6. **Meditation**

Meditation has been shown to reduce stress and anxiety, as it allows us to calm our thoughts and focus on the present moment. Regular meditation practice can improve our ability to focus and concentrate, as it strengthens the neural pathways in our brains that are responsible for attention and cognitive control.

It can help us develop greater self-awareness, as it allows us to observe our thoughts and emotions without judgment. This can empower us to gain insight into our patterns of thinking and behavior and make positive changes in our lives. Regular meditation practice has been shown to increase positive emotions such as happiness and contentment and decrease negative emotions such as anger and fear.

Meditation has also been linked to physical health benefits, such as reduced blood pressure, improved immune function, and decreased inflammation.

Overall, meditation is a powerful tool for improving our mental and physical well-being. By incorporating a regular meditation practice into our daily lives, we can reduce stress, improve focus and concentration, and cultivate greater self-awareness and emotional well-being.

Find a quiet and comfortable space. Choose a quiet space where you can sit comfortably without distractions. You can sit on a cushion or a chair with your back straight, your shoulders relaxed, and your feet flat on the floor.

Choose a focus: You can choose a focus for your meditation practice, such as your breath, a mantra, or a visualization. The breath is a common focus for beginners, as it is always with us and can serve as an anchor to the present moment.

Set a timer: Set a timer for a desired length of time, such as 5 or 10 minutes, to help you stay focused and avoid the temptation to check the time.

Close your eyes and breathe: Close your eyes and take a few deep breaths to help you relax. Then, begin to focus your attention on your chosen focus. If your mind wanders, simply bring your attention back to your focus without judgment.

Practice regularly: Consistency is key when it comes to meditation. Try to practice every day, even if it's just for a few minutes at a time.

Experiment with different techniques and find what works best for you. With practice, you can develop a deeper sense of calm, clarity, and well-being in your daily life.

7. **Prayer**

For many people, prayer is a way to connect with a higher power or divine energy. This can provide a sense of comfort and support and help them feel less alone in the world. Prayer can be a way to express gratitude and appreciation for the blessings in our lives. By acknowledging the good things, we have, we can cultivate a sense of abundance and joy.

Prayer can be a source of hope and healing, particularly during difficult times. It can provide a sense of comfort and peace and help us feel more resilient in the face of adversity. It can also be a way to reflect on our thoughts, feelings, and beliefs and gain insight into our inner world. By taking time to connect with ourselves, we can develop greater self-awareness and self-understanding.

Offering prayers can be a powerful tool for spiritual growth, personal development, and connection with a higher power. By incorporating prayer into our daily lives, we can cultivate a deeper sense of meaning, purpose, and well-being.

Jiya: This is soul-stirring, Maya. Until today, I was considering prayers as the only foundation of spirituality. My heartfelt gratitude for being my mentor and guiding me through the fundamentals of life You have not only saved my marriage but also transformed me into a better version of myself, and I assure you, this version will keep getting enriched day by day. I am going to remember this trek for the rest of my life.

Maya- I laud your commitment. I feel grateful that I am able to drive a change in your life. Also, I thank you for the opportunity to share my learning. In your company, days flew by as if they had wings. I wish the trek would have been a little longer.

Voila, I can see the Bali Pass Camp; I think it is not farther than 100 meters. Just a couple of more steps, and we are there. I will miss these snowstorms, which have beaten the coolest air conditioner ever designed by mankind. I will miss these walks in the clouds, which are alien in the plains, and most of all, I will miss the joy of seeing all 12 peers make it to the whopping great pass.

As the team reaches, Jayesh gathers everyone for a short huddle.

Jayesh- First of all, clap for yourselves to have made it to the destination. You guys have great wits.

What you see ahead is the Bali Pass Summit, which we shall mount tomorrow at 3 a.m. So, you better finish your meals and dive into your camps for a good night's sleep.

The moment Jayesh completes his last words of advice, the storm gains more momentum, as if waiting for all the members to reach him. In a jiffy, they take off their backpacks and set up their tents.

The weather outside is frightful, but the inside is delightful. Despite the day's tough hike, everyone seems refreshed and electrified to reach the summit the next morning.

Chapter 9

LIFE IS A TREK OF CHEER

"Carpe Diem. Seize the day, boys. Make your lives extraordinary."

– Robin Williams

At 2:55 am, everyone assembles with their head torches on. Last night, there was a fresh spell of snowfall, but now the sparkling stars forecast clear weather.

Jayesh (while massaging his chin): Wait, there seems to be one member missing... Maya.

Everyone turns around, but there is no sign of the absent member.

Jiya: When I woke up, Maya was not in the camp. So, I thought she might have gotten up early, as she does. I could not see her even after I packed the camp. Even her backpack was not there.

Vivaan (another team member) (pointing in a direction with narrowed eyes)—I think that's her.

A head was seesawing while approaching them, and everyone's eyes were fixed with amazement.

As Maya covers a distance, she waves her hand and gestures an apology.

Maya: Sorry guys, you had to wait for me.

Jayesh, but where were you? We thought the other day's boar had kidnapped you.

Maya (with a broad chuckle) After sleeping for 2 hours, I woke at 12 a.m. I felt so fresh and thrilled about the day's trek that I jumped out of the quilt and stepped into my shoes. Zipping my bag, I gripped my walking stick and patrolled out to gaze at the beauty of nature and click some pictures.

Megha (as if thunderstruck) It means you hardly slept a wink, and you have been on the prowl for three hours. What if some snow leopard had zeroed in on you for his breakfast?

Jiya: This is Maya; she knows very well how to take on challenges head-on.

Jayesh-Amigos, if you are done with your cackles, can we please move along as we are already late by 10 minutes?

From the bird's-eye view, it seems like some fireflies have formed a queue in the trajectory of the peak. The uphill on the edge is menacing, as even a slight fall could swirl the hiker to the starting point.

However, they complete the trek of pride safely and reach the summit. As they raise their hands with radiant smiles, the first ray of the sun showers on the peak, as if welcoming the champions. For everyone, this has been the best morning of their lives at this height of over 16,000 feet. They jump, hug, and cheer each other on. This is followed by some emotional speeches with tears and sobs. As the waves of sentiments lessen, they all sit facing the sun, expressing gratitude for this unspeakable joy.

The same morning, they begin their descent at 8 a.m. and reach the Sankri village before dusk.

Before departing, Jiya asks for everyone's attention, jawing, "Guys, let's get an earful of Maya's departing words."

Maya (with a smug look): Well, there are many lessons of life to share, but here's what I have to say about women's empowerment.

Walk your talk

Maya: Since childhood, we have been fed with women's empowerment, but more often than not, it is limited to a wholesome recipe of discussion. As we speak, 130 million girls remain out of school worldwide. 1 in 9 girls under the age of 18 experience sexual abuse or assault by an adult. 12 million girls under 18 are married each year. Only 3 in 9 managers or supervisors are women, but we have a fine tooth for talking about women's equality.

At the same time, there are some fighter women who, instead of chin-wagging, rose against injustice.

On June 16, 1963, Valentina Tereshkova was the first woman to go to space, fighting for women's rights to participate in STEM. On January 4, 2007, Nancy Pelosi was elected the first female Speaker of the House of Representatives, proving women should also hold high leadership roles in politics.

Sojourner Truth was an African-American abolitionist who was born into slavery. In 1828, she became the first black woman to win a custody court battle against a white man, and she was able to recover her son from slavery. At the Ohio Women's Rights Convention of 1851, Truth delivered a speech titled "Ain't I a Woman?" that stirred hearts and became widely told during the Civil War era.

In 2012, at the age of 15, Malala Yousafzai was shot in the head by the Taliban in Pakistan. The shooting attempt was a response to her stance on the right of girls to gain an education after the Taliban had banned them from attending school. She is now one of the world's most iconic female change agents, and in 2014, she became the youngest-ever Nobel Peace Prize laureate.

Pelin Aslantaş is the only woman bus driver among 202 male drivers in Edirne, Turkey. Her mother taught her how to drive.

There are scores of such examples where, instead of becoming a part of the herd, women rebelled against societal norms. Therefore, we too must walk our talk.

What can we do at the individual level to abolish women's inequality?

There are several ways that we can brush off female injustice. Here are some suggestions:

Raise Awareness: The first step is to raise awareness that gender inequality is like a venomous weed in our society. We pray to Goddess Lakshmi for wealth, Goddess Saraswati for knowledge, and Goddess Kali for strength. But the irony is, we mistreat the woman at home, the one who is the binding force in our family. Therefore, we need to educate people about the inequalities and injustices that women face in our society.

Change begins at home: Our upbringing defines our culture, ethics, and individualism. We should encourage our boys from a young age to respect all women. We should train them to do their chores and to lend a helping hand at home and in the kitchen. If these are ingrained in them at a very young age in kids, then their mindset gets attuned to the positive direction. We will surely create a happy and healthy environment.

Encourage Gender Equality at Home: We can start by modeling gender equality in our own homes. This can include sharing household responsibilities, treating each other with respect, and promoting gender-neutral language and behaviors.

Speak Out: Even in this smart age, we see women and even girl kids becoming victims of heinous crimes. And most of them do not ever get reported. We need to speak out against female injustice when we see it happening. We can do this by confronting individuals who engage in sexist behavior or language and by reporting incidents of discrimination and harassment to authorities.

Support Women's Organizations: There are many organizations that work to promote gender equality and women's rights. Supporting these organizations financially or by volunteering can be a great way to help fight female injustice.

Educate ourselves: We need to educate ourselves about the issues that women face. This can include reading books and articles about gender inequality, attending workshops or seminars, and taking courses on women's studies.

Advocate for Policy Changes: We can advocate for policy changes that promote gender equality, such as equal pay laws and laws against discrimination in the workplace. We can also vote for political candidates who support these policies.

Support Women in Leadership: Women are often underrepresented in leadership roles. We can support women who are running for political office, in leadership positions in the workplace, or who are starting their own businesses.

Fighting female injustice is an ongoing effort that requires the involvement and support of everyone.

However, these suggestions may sound easier said than done. Therefore, I have founded an NGO for women's empowerment, **Radical Change**. There are hundreds of women and even some men volunteering across the country. We have helped thousands of unprivileged women battle against injustice and savor life. We have rescued several women working as sex workers and empowered them to venture into startups. The NGO offers skill training, wherein reputed professionals initiate the workshops. So, this is my little step to drive radical change, and this foundation will gain more momentum as more people rope in.

Jiya: This is phenomenal, Maya. Unlike most of us, you are a doer. I am eager to contribute to this cause, so please also count me in as a classical dance teacher.

Here's a short story for you that is the sum and substance of everything I have shared on this trip.

Life is a great opportunity to cheer

Once upon a time, in ancient China, there lived three old monks. Their names are not remembered today simply because they never revealed them to anybody in China; they are simply known as the three laughing monks. They always traveled together and did nothing else but laugh.

The monks would enter a village or town, stand in the center of its main square, and laugh slowly but surely. The people who lived and worked there and the passersby couldn't resist and had to start laughing as well until a small laughing crowd had formed. Eventually, the laughter would spread to the whole town. That was the moment when the three old monks moved on to the next village. Their laughter was their only prayer and all of their teaching because they never spoke to anybody. They just created that situation all over China. As the news about the monks spread, they were loved and respected. People had never known such spiritual teachers before or after.

The trio seemed to communicate that life should be taken only as a great opportunity to laugh, as if they had discovered some kind of cosmic joke. So, they traveled and laughed for many years, making the people contagious with their laughter throughout China. This continued until one day, while being at a particular village in the northern province, one of them died. People were shocked and came running from afar, leaving the fields unattended for the day, only to witness the other two monks' reaction to this dramatic event. They were expecting them to show sorrow or even cry. The whole village came to the place where the three monks were—two alive and one dead.

However, the two remaining monks were laughing even harder. They were laughing and laughing, and they could not seem to stop. So, a few of the good people who were assisting at this scene in this belief approached them and asked why they weren't mourning at all for their deceased friend.

Then, for one time, the monks responded, "Because yesterday on our way to your village, he proposed the bet on who of us would beat the other two and die first, and now he has won, the old rogue. He even had a testament prepared. It is about the tradition of washing the dead and changing his clothes before putting him on the funeral pyre. But the old monk had explicitly asked to leave the old clothes on him, as he had never been filthy for one day. "I never allowed any of the filth of this world to reach me through my laughter." His testament stated that his body should be placed on the pyre with the garments he was wearing."

As the fire was lit and it started licking on his clothes, to everyone's astonishment, suddenly fireworks of a hundred colors went exploding up and down and in all directions. Finally, the people who had gathered there also joined the laughter of the two wise men.

The only reason that we are here on this earth is so we can laugh and laugh and never stop experiencing jubilation. So, the next time you face a problem, look in the mirror and just laugh the problem away because your joy is what makes you alive.

After a few moments of muteness, everyone bursts into a sidesplitter, and a hoot of laughter echoes in the glaciated valley.

Maya, friends, let's tag along for another trek, maybe in the next year, with new challenges and new self-realizations.

"Indeed, we shall stay connected and hook up for our next adventure," everyone affirms before departing.

www.ingramcontent.com/pod-product-compliance
Lightning Source LLC
LaVergne TN
LVHW091103150826
845673LV00002B/701

* 9 7 9 8 8 9 1 3 3 9 5 1 4 *